SPEEDBUMPS

SPEEDBUMPS

Flooring It Through Hollywood

Teri Garr

with Henriette Mantel

HUDSON
STREET
PRESS

HUDSON STREET PRESS
Published by Penguin Group
Penguin Group (USA) Inc., 375 Hudson Street, New York 10014, U.S.A.
Penguin Group (Canada), 90 Eglinton Avenue East, Suite 700, Toronto, Ontario, Canada M4P 2Y3
(a division of Pearson Penguin Canada Inc.)
Penguin Books Ltd, 80 Strand, London WC2R 0RL, England
Penguin Ireland, 25 St. Stephen's Green, Dublin 2, Ireland (a division of Penguin Books Ltd.)
Penguin Group (Australia), 250 Camberwell Road, Camberwell, Victoria 3124, Australia
(a division of Pearson Australia Group Pty. Ltd.)
Penguin Books India Pvt. Ltd., 11 Community Centre, Panchsheel Park, New Delhi – 110 017, India
Penguin Books (NZ), cnr Airborne and Rosedale Roads, Albany, Auckland 1310, New Zealand
(a division of Pearson New Zealand Ltd.)
Penguin Books (South Africa) (Pty.) Ltd., 24 Sturdee Avenue, Rosebank, Johannesburg 2196, South Africa

Penguin Books Ltd., Registered Offices: 80 Strand, London WC2R 0RL, England

First published by Hudson Street Press, a member of Penguin Group (USA) Inc.

First Printing, November 2005
10 9 8 7 6 5 4 3 2 1

Copyright © Teri Garr, 2005
All rights reserved

Photo credits: Photos 1–13, 15–19, 21, 25, 28–32, 35, 37, 39–41, 43–49 courtesy of Teri Garr. Photo 14 courtesy of *Pajama Party* © 1964 Orion Pictures Distribution Corporation. Photo 20 courtesy of Universal Studios Licensing LLLP. Photo 22 courtesy of Blye/Beard Productions, Apls Productions, and the Beneficiaries of the Estate of Sonny Bono. Photos 23 and 24 courtesy of *Young Frankenstein* © 1974 Twentieth Century Fox. Photo 26 courtesy of *Oh, God!* © Warner Bros. Inc. Photo 27 courtesy of *Close Encounters of the Third Kind* © 1977 Columbia Pictures Industries, Inc. Courtesy of Columbia Pictures. Photo 33 courtesy of *Tootsie* © 1977 Columbia Pictures Industries, Inc. Courtesy of Columbia Pictures. Photo 34 reprinted by permission of *Ms. Magazine* © 1983. Photo 36 © Schillervision. Photo 38 courtesy of *Mr. Mom* © 1983 Orion Pictures Distribution Corporation. Photo 42 courtesy of *Waiting for the Light* © 1990 Orion Pictures Distribution Corporation. Photo 50 © Silvia Mautner, (310) 836-9900.

All rights reserved.

HUDSON STREET PRESS   REGISTERED TRADEMARK—MARCA REGISTRADA

CIP data is available.
ISBN 1-594-63007-0

Printed in the United States of America
Set in Horley Old Style Regular
Designed by Leonard Telesca

This book is printed on acid-free paper. ♾

For Molly

Contents

CONTENTS

I like to drive fast. Not dangerously, mind you. But I still like to head west on Sunset Boulevard toward my house, hitting all the green lights. Needless to say, I've never been a huge fan of speed-bumps. Who is? As far as I'm concerned, they're needless obstacles stuck in the road to slow you down. That doesn't really work for me. Ever since I was a kid I've always been in a hurry to get someplace. I never slowed down. I've flown over some small bumps and some big ones and some that tore the muffler off the bottom of my car. But lately I've started to wonder—what was the rush? Someone put those speedbumps there for a reason. So these days, when I come to a speedbump, I just slow down, roll over it gently, and keep going. And that, to me, is what life is. Full speed ahead, slow down for the bump, and then it's back to pedal-to-the-metal.

As a California girl, I've always been into cars. Maybe it was growing up with older brothers. I'd wander into the garage to find them staring silently into the open hood of our '52 Ford as if it were the Notre Dame cathedral. I shared their reverence for the auto. Cars were all about action, momentum, and, I suspect, sex. (More on sex later.) Most of my life has been about show business, but what I've come to realize in writing this book is that the underlying story is about movement, action, and endless propulsion forward. In my family, we always just kept going and going.

Whether it was in a car, in school, or in ballet classes, I spent much of my childhood trying to get somewhere. I've lost count of how many times my mother would throw my two brothers and me in the family station wagon to drive from L.A. to the East Coast and back again. My mom would announce that my vaudevillian dad wanted us with him and we'd hit the road. The back end of our station wagon would be stacked high with suitcases, books, peanut-butter sandwiches, and the empty birdcage of our two parakeets, Bee and Joe, who would flit about freely inside the car. Wherever we landed—New Jersey, Cleveland, Timbuktu— we'd find a friend or relative who had room for us. There we would make a home until my dad got yet another job on the other end of the country, and off we would go again.

By the time I started to dance professionally and, later, to act, first in television, then in movies, I was used to momentum as a way of life. No matter what I accomplished or where I was, I was always focused on the next job. Full speed ahead. This served me well as an actress. I was comfortable flying from California to places all over the world to work for a month or three. At least in airplanes I never woke up with my hair stuck in one of my brothers' peanut-butter sandwiches. And moving fast felt familiar. If a job came in, I was always ready to pick up and scramble to the next place, just like I did when I was a kid.

Recently, I've been traveling again, sometimes with my eleven-year-old daughter and sometimes alone. But this time around it's a little different. Now I don't have to wait for my appearances to be transferred to celluloid and distributed on movie screens across the country. Instead, I travel all over the country to talk to people about living with multiple sclerosis. For the first time in my life as a performer I talk directly to my audience, both in groups and individually, about living with this scum-sucking pig of a disease. (And I mean that in the nicest possible way.) My audiences still seem happy to see me but, now more than ever, I'm happy to see them, too.

Sometimes when I'm on the road now I see what hardships really are, both for myself and for the people I talk to. But the big thing I've learned as I approach the wise old age of thirty (oh, ha-ha!) is that physical speedbumps can always be surpassed. The real obstacles are emotional and mental. Life's toughest challenge is in finding a way to move past those hurdles to find joy.

My body has given me a great life so far. Now it's time for my mind and spirit to return the favor. Flooring it over the speedbumps isn't always wise. I've had my share of whiplash, and I'm sure I should have been a little more cautious, but like my mom always said, "Ve git too soon old unt too late schmart."

So I keep moving, speedbumps and all, and I hope you enjoy the ride I'm about to share.

Thanks,
Teri

I

Hollywood: This Mess Is a Place

On March 29, 1982, the day of the Academy Awards, I woke up excited and ready to go to the Oscars for the first time in my life (I'd always watched them on TV, like everyone else). It was a perfect day in L.A., the kind of beautiful day any self-respecting Los Angeleno takes for granted. Outside my window the skies were blue, and a hummingbird flirted with the lemon tree.

But that day was different. I had been nominated for an Academy Award for my performance as Sandy Lester, Dustin Hoffman's neurotic, struggling-actress girlfriend, in *Tootsie*. Under Sydney Pollack's direction, *Tootsie* had been a runaway hit, starring Dustin as an unemployed actor who pretends to be a woman in order to land a role on a soap opera.

I couldn't believe my good fortune; I had been really, truly nominated, like all my big-screen idols—Ginger Rogers, Shirley MacLaine, and Geraldine Page. The nomination also officially

1

made me a member of the illustrious Academy of Motion Picture Arts and Sciences, which offered major perks, such as getting free copies of the nominated films every year, screening invites and voting privileges. I was proud. The Academy not only knew I existed, they thought I was good!

I tried to sleep in, but by eight o'clock I couldn't fight the excitement any longer. I pulled myself out of bed, my mind moving faster than my body in contemplation of the major issues of the day: my hair, makeup, and dress, all of which ranked right up there with the Cold War, at least on that special day. But the first order of business: the gym.

I went to Jane Fonda's Workout Studio on Robertson in Beverly Hills. I figured I'd go for the burn before I went for the gold. And so I worked out and exhausted myself, but still didn't put a dent in my hyperexcitement. Even though I'd grown up around movie sets and actors, my nomination brought with it the magic that bridged the gap between the ordinary and the fantasy, and I was buying into it. Why not? I rushed home to start my toilette.

By the time I pulled my silver Mercedes back into the driveway, my stylists had arrived at my Laurel Canyon home. Nowadays stars are styled by those who are fashionistas in their own right, but back then I turned to the hair and makeup people I was working with on the set of my next movie, *Mr. Mom*. Like the movie crews I'd grown up around, Bob Mills and Jamie Smith were two down-to-earth craftsmen who, like me, were from the San Fernando Valley. I knew I could trust them.

Bob was no small talent in the world of makeup. (He'd later go on to work with Glenn Close for years.) After he created my look, it was Jamie's turn to do my hair. I watched him stagger through the front door under the weight of a vast trunk, which I assumed contained various high-tech hairstyling instruments. I would soon learn, however, that there was only one high-volume secret to his art: a tub of gel.

Serious as a surgeon, Jamie wasted no time. That's what I liked about him. So practical, so reliable. So, shall we say, gay? Jamie sat me down at my dining-room table. There was no mirror in front of me like there would be at the salon, but what could possibly go wrong? Jamie was a man of few words, and I, by contrast, was so intensely excited I felt like I was hovering two feet above the chair. So for the next three hours I blathered on about who might win what while he yanked my hair with such force that I felt as if I'd gotten a face-lift as a bonus. After a flurry of twirling, curling, blowing, teasing, and enough Aquanet to permanently damage the ozone layer, he released me from the chair to see the results of his handiwork in the bathroom mirror.

My long, blond locks rose high around my head like the feathers of a peacock. It was a gravitational feat. A masterpiece.

It had taken me forever to find the perfect dress to wear to the Awards. In those days, the designers and jewelers didn't just call you up and volunteer to lend you their million-dollar one-of-a-kind haute couture extravaganzas. Back then, you actually had to go out and schlep around, looking for a dress like everybody else—or at least pay someone to do it for you. (Searching for the perfect Oscar frock made me think of the wedding dress I never planned to shop for.) I looked until I was dizzy at all the usual places on Rodeo Drive: Valentino, Gucci, Saks. I finally decided on a black, capped-sleeve, floor-length dress from Neiman Marcus, which was slit up the side to show my legs. It was covered with sparkling jewels, boasted the requisite five-inch-thick shoulder pads, and was the newest look from the hot designer Frabrice.

Ever hear of him?

Exactly.

The dress uniquely captured that timeless *Dynasty* look. My boyfriend at the time, Roger Birnbaum, an aspiring producer who would later go on to develop such films as *The Sixth Sense*, *Seabiscuit*, and *Rain Man*, looked positively dignified in his freshly rented tux, and I looked like a Linda Evans wannabe. I know that styles change, and fashion is ephemeral. But looking back, I'll tell you one thing: Hideous is forever.

At this point you'd be wise to ask, "What the hell were you thinking? Why didn't anyone stop you?" But you needed to live it to know: It was like *Invasion of the Body Snatchers.* We were *all* in the same *Dynasty*-induced, shoulder-padded, zombie-eyed haze.

With all the spraying and primping and wrestling myself into my dress, before I knew it, it was 2 P.M. and my limo had arrived. My mother, my brothers Ed and Phil, and my sister-in-law Bunny showed up at the door to take pictures, as if Roger and I were heading off to the prom. After a few obligatory snapshots, I dispensed my well-practiced air kisses, and off we went.

Maybe I was on my way to collect my statuette . . . Who knew?

The rest of that day and evening is pretty much a blur now— the adrenaline-fueled trip down the red carpet, the interviews with Siskel and Ebert, the blinding flashes of hundreds of cameras as the photographers shouted, "Teri! Over here! Over here!" Just about the only thing I'm sure really happened is that the paparazzi confused me with Joe Namath. Who could blame them? Those shoulder pads!

All the photos of me from the red carpet that day show the same great big grin. I was happy inside, but also wired. Years of hard work had finally come together in one auspicious achievement. Like any little girl who's ever dreamed of a career in show business, I'd imagined this moment a few million times, except in my daydreams I was usually wearing a better dress. And now, here I was, and the dress really didn't matter.

Roger and I made our way down the red carpet, chatting with the TV reporters and with other nominees like Peter O'Toole and Jack Lemmon. At one point, Meryl Streep, who was nominated for Best Actress in *Sophie's Choice,* turned to me and said, "Isn't this exciting?" And, just as you'd expect from a clever comedienne, I responded, "Yeah, I guess so."

I was so excited that I was unexcited.

By the time Roger and I took our seats in the theater, I was a nervous mess. Best Supporting Actress was my category, and one of the first ones up, so, luckily, I didn't have long to wait. The show zipped along for what seemed like thirty-six hours, but was really only about four minutes. Then, finally . . . Next up, Best Supporting Actress.

My co-star, Jessica Lange (it's okay if you haven't heard of her) was also nominated for Best Supporting Actress in *Tootsie.* It's not unusual for two actors in the same film to be nominated for the same award—it's happened throughout Oscar history, from *The Godfather* (James Caan, Robert Duvall, and Al Pacino were all nominated for Best Supporting Actor) to *Chicago* (both Queen Latifah and Catherine Zeta-Jones were nominated for Best Supporting Actress). But this time it was happening to me. The others nominated in my category were Kim Stanley for *Frances,* Lesley Ann Warren for *Victor/Victoria,* and Glenn Close for *The World According to Garp.* I figured Glenn Close would win, and not just because Jessica and I would split the *Tootsie* vote. I thought she was perfect in *Garp* as Garp's nurse mother. And after all, I was the girl who'd danced in Elvis movies. I'd been buried in sand for an Annette Funicello movie. Was I really going to win an Academy Award? Well, yes . . . maybe.

When the envelope was opened, my heart stopped.

"And the winner is . . . Jessica Lange."

I instantly smiled, bigger perhaps than I've ever smiled before. I may have played the Statue of Liberty on roller skates once, but I'm no fool—while the winner is adjusting her girdle and kissing everyone within a ten-person radius, the camera is always on the losers. Of course, the movie *The Oscar* with Stephen Boyd came to mind.

Was it the insufferable Jessica Lange's impeccable timing that won her Best Supporting Actress? (Incidentally, I thought she was very nice until she won the Oscar and I didn't. Nothing personal.) Or was it a sympathy vote? She'd been nominated for Best Actress for *Frances,* in which she was brilliant, but there was no way anybody was going to beat Meryl Streep in *Sophie's Choice.* Maybe it was the fact that she was much, much older than me? Who knows?

At any rate, the pressure was off me, way off. I took some comfort in the fact that just a few days earlier the *Washington Post* had said that I was "Not quite the girl next door; that would be too perfect. She's more like the girl next door to the girl next door." I wasn't sure what that meant, but I figured it was too much of a stretch for the girl next door to the girl next door to win an Academy Award.

So, I didn't win. I fell back on the old adage "being nominated is just as good as winning." I had a fabulous view of the ceremony, I was invited to all the big after-parties. I'd worked my ass off to get here, and I didn't want to miss a second of it, even the bad hors d'oeuvres. It wasn't my style to fixate on the loss for too long, and I had my life pretty much in perspective: I was a successful actress. I was making movies—good movies, if I do say so myself. I was working with the best directors in the business—Francis Ford Coppola, Sydney Pollack, and Steven Spielberg. I was living the life I'd dreamed of . . . I was on top of the world, and nothing was going to get in the way of that, especially the loss of an Academy Award to what's-her-name.

When the lights went up, Roger and I went out to retrieve our car from the valets. So did everyone else. Win or lose, star or not, you wait for your car with everyone else, and waiting for your car is a drag. But we finally got out of the Dorothy Chandler Pavilion and drove to superagent Swifty Lazar's party at the famous Beverly Hills restaurant Spago. There I was, in a fabulous dress that would be hot for at least another thirty seconds, riding in a limo to the most fabled celebrity haunt in town, toasting my director, the esteemed Sydney Pollack, and rubbing elbows with every movie star who was hot at the time. I felt as frothy and as light and flowing as . . . my hair. I was also planning to knock back a few. I *am* Irish, after all.

Champagne flowed late into the night, and by the time I got home, my family (who, for some strange reason, had stayed at my place to watch the show) was gone. On the top of an empty pizza box they had written, "Win or lose, we love you anyway." But there wasn't time to linger in my near-perfect glory. I had work the next day—I was shooting *Mr. Mom,* playing the mom to Michael Keaton's Mr.—and as the lead, calling in sick wasn't an option.

So I crawled into bed with Roger and closed my eyes. I wondered what Lesley Ann Warren was thinking. After all, we all must have thought we were going to win at some point. Oscar or no Oscar, I had a boyfriend sleeping next to me. My career was blazing. I had a sweet house in the Hollywood Hills. I was a regular on *The Tonight Show* and *Late Night with David Letterman*. I was on the cover of *Ms.* magazine, and in *The New Yorker* Pauline Kael, one of my heroes, said I had "become the funniest neurotic dizzy dame on the screen." It took me all of five minutes to put the loss of the Oscar into perspective. Life was good.

I sure made it look easy, didn't I?

I thought it would be simple from then on. I was a working actress, and in my mind all was going according to plan. But it ain't always so, is it? My body had a trick or two up its sleeve. A stumble here, a tingling finger there. I was trained as a dancer and knew better than to indulge the random aches and pains that visited now and then. Being a successful Hollywood actress may be challenging, but little did I know that the very body that had always been my calling card would betray me.

The biggest challenges of my life were still ahead.

2

Daddy Dearest, Hold Your Applause

I was born into a gypsy showbiz family on a day sometime in the middle of the twentieth century. (My mother taught me that showbiz people never tell their real ages. She never revealed hers or my father's. When he passed away and I read his obituary, I noticed that it said he was about five years younger than he really was. I mentioned this to my mother. I said, "Mom, why did you lie about his age? He's dead. Nobody's going to hire him now." She said, "Dear, we're in show business. We never tell our real age.")

When I was born my father, Eddie Garr, who was a comedian, had a job performing in a USO show in Guam, of all places, where he'd somehow managed to break his back falling out of an open jeep (or maybe off a bar stool). My mother, Phyllis "Legs" Lind Garr, was already single-handedly raising two boys—my brothers, six-year-old Ed and two-year-old Phil. Needless to say, my arrival in 19?? wasn't met with fireworks. I was just an add-on to an already hectic, seat-of-the-pants operation.

My father, when he wasn't doing time entertaining the armed forces, was doing time entertaining the masses. He was a very funny, semifamous, vaudevillian, alcoholic, Irish comedian—not necessarily in that order. Oh, and he was also rather fond of gambling, but who's counting? From pictures I can tell he was very dashing, with his "black Irish" complexion. I barely knew the man, and he died when I was eleven. But over the years, I would hear that he was funny.

It's a strange way to learn about your father, from the Hall of Fame of comedians. They all said, "Eddie Garr, oh yeah. *He* was funny." In 1983 when Jackie Gleason played my father in *The Sting II,* he said, "Eddie Garr, helluva guy! I used to go watch him perform over at the Fort Lee Club in Jersey." Jerry Stiller once told me, "I worked with your dad once, great guy." So although my father had three kids he barely ever saw, a gambling habit to make Bugsy Siegel proud, and a lifelong affair with the bottle, apparently he was funny. I guess I had to get it from somewhere.

Then again, that's assuming that I'm funny. I forgot to ask Jackie Gleason what he thought about that.

If my father was known for being funny, my mother was known for her legs. My mother's legs were so fabulous, her friends used to call her "Legs Lind." I still have a nylon-stocking ad that she did in the '30s for a fashion magazine. It showed only her legs, but she cherished it—she kept it for years, carefully stored in its plastic covering, and would tell me proudly, "I got that job because I had the best legs in New York City." (How could I prove she was wrong? I wasn't there for the voting.) So, back in the 1930s, my mother did what any dancer with the best legs in New York City would do: She became a Rockette at Radio City Music Hall. Soon after, in 1934, she met my father, who was ten years her senior, when they were both cast in *Strike Me Pink* with Jimmy Durante on Broadway. They fell in love, got married, and somehow managed to have three kids. My brother Ed was the oldest; Phil, the classic middle child; and I, the baby darling.

Shortly after I was born, my father came home to California from Guam. He'd been gone only a few months, but long enough to miss my first entrance. From then on, we were always on the move, hardly stopping anywhere for longer than a year or two. Believe me, it was a pieced-together life. From Hollywood to Cleveland to New York—wherever my father found work, my mother would pack us up to follow. Despite the fact that my mother really did want us to have a stable childhood, she was determined to chase after my father. She was just crazy about him. She would always say, "Your dad wants us there," and even though it seemed he never gave a hoot about where we were, she was determined to keep our little family together. We drove from city to city, back and forth across the country, in a green Ford station wagon with wood paneling, instead of the red Town and Country with wood paneling that I would have preferred (those were for rich people).

When I was five years old, we moved into my grandfather's house in Cleveland. The house was a duplex, and we lived in the attic. I call those my Anne Frank years, no disrespect intended. We weren't exactly hiding in unmitigated terror from a fascist regime, but still, it was a pretty small attic.

My dad was working off and on, so my mother had to be frugal. Lucky for us, she could figure out a practical use for anything, and she was proud to tell the world: Our car boasted a bumper sticker that read, THIS CAR STOPS AT ALL GARAGE SALES. It was no lie. Once, she picked up an ugly ten-cent syrup jug and said, "This could be a lamp." And, presto, it was. She was always inventing, making something out of nothing. If I wanted a new toy, she would look at a pile of rocks on the ground and say, "I think you could make a dollhouse out of those rocks over there." One Mother's Day I gave her a jar of rocks and told her they were a bouquet of flowers.

When my dad was on the vaudeville or nightclub wheel, he was always looking for the next job. When business was good, one show would lead to the next, so he was often on the road to another gig, whether it was in Philly, Manhattan, or Chicago. He was never around and, in the way kids do, I knew there was something missing in my family—I just wasn't sure what.

One Sunday morning, after he came home from a road trip, we three kids climbed into our parents' bed, all at once, to wake them up. There we were, the whole family, in their big double bed, laughing, talking, and, of course, jumping. Suddenly, the bed (which had probably been picked up secondhand at a garage sale) broke, and we all went crashing to the floor in a heap.

It was a rare moment that held a feeling of love and completeness, and I specifically remember thinking, This is happiness. Believe me, plenty of kids have had it way worse than I did—we were basically normal, neither lacking nor privileged. But in the bedlam of that bed, I recognized a family life that I'd yearned for without even knowing it was missing. That's probably why I've been looking for happiness in beds ever since.

From there, it was from my grandfather's duplex in Cleveland to my aunt Terry's colonial in New Jersey, and then, again, back West. On our return to California we moved into a nice house in the San Fernando Valley. I was eight; Ike was president. (Do the math.) My brothers and I went to Riverside School, a true Southern California–style cluster of bungalows, where the other girls and I used to sit on the steps of the buildings and polish our nails and be smartasses.

I was already emerging as a bit of a showbiz brat. Whenever there was a group picture I always wanted to be front and center. My teacher, Mr. Slifkin, used to tease me, saying, "Boy, Miss Terry Ann Garr sure did want to be in that picture." At the end of fourth grade, he handed me a note that said, "Dear Terry, someday you will be a great comedienne. Love, Mr. Slifkin."

I have saved this note in my box of keepsakes ever since. I was already figuring out who I would be, and Mr. Slifkin was one of the first adults to notice. With this little bit of recognition came the first hint of ambition. Maybe he was right. Maybe I could become a comedienne, even though I wasn't sure what that was.

That was in the San Fernando Valley, the neighborhood I loved and felt most comfortable in. Our house was on Houston Street in North Hollywood; in those days, lots of people who worked in the studios as craftsmen, musicians, and makeup artists lived there. These days, North Hollywood is the porn capital of the world. But at the time it was a nice, comfy, middle-class neighborhood that featured a maze of sidewalks on which to skate and loads of kids to play with. My best friends were Sharon Costello, Linda Marchese, and Joyce von Herzen, three girls my age who lived on my block. (Mom used to brag that there were twenty-three kids on our block alone. She was pretty proud of herself for having found such a wholesome, normal, kid-friendly neighborhood. Of course, just because there were a lot of kids and families on our block didn't mean everything was cool. I'm sure there was a lot going on behind closed doors . . . our own family's included. The dad of my best friend ended up going to "the big house," even though he was a nice guy. My mom must have thought, If these

13

people can pull it off, so can I. I suppose those fifties gals were all in the same boat. Misery loves company, as they say.) Together, my friends and I built tree houses and played with baby dolls that my mother made out of old socks. It was at that house, my favorite house, that I started to notice that my father was around a little more. Except now that he was home, he was in bed a lot.

I didn't know what was wrong with him. Looking back, maybe it was one continuous hangover, but I never thought that at the time. He was also in and out of the hospital a fair amount, which I knew was more serious than nursing the hair of the dog. When my father was sick, my friends and I were told to play quietly. My mother was forever saying, "Your dad is sleeping. Don't make any noise; don't play outside his window." My favorite place to play? Outside his window, on the big porch of our house. So while my father lay sick in bed, my girlfriends and I played house outside his window. We took care of our baby dolls, never mentioning our husbands, whom we pretended were either off fighting in a war or just plain dead. It was us girls and our babies, cooking dinner and having fun. No boys allowed.

My mother did her best to hold the family together. She took a job as an instructor at a local knit shop to help pay the bills. (My Austrian grandmother had taught her girls to sew, knit, and crochet, but apparently not how to pick a man.) Mom saw to it that we were always clothed and fed, but our household was perpetually disorganized and chaotic. Sometimes both of our parents were working and, without money for what we'd call childcare today, we were left to fend for ourselves. Even though we didn't lock the door in those days, we were kind of like latchkey kids, long before that term was ever used.

And yet my mother didn't know all our tricks. As she backed down the driveway in our family car, she would shout, "You kids be good, and whatever you do, don't go on the roof." Of course, as soon as she was out of sight, we'd climb right up onto the roof. That's what kids do (except for my daughter, who's perfect). But for the most part, being left alone was not a big deal. Like all kids, I enjoyed not being told what to do. I also liked to play pretend-mommy. Sometimes I would bake "cakes," put a little bit of every-thing (like baking soda, flour, milk, eggs, raisins, graham crackers, chocolate pudding, Crisco, cornmeal, and, of course, rice, cheese, and hot dogs) into a bowl and bake it in the oven. The "cakes" turned out like bricks with big holes in them, which had to be buried in the backyard. (Ah, the joy of cooking.) When I realized that our house was a wreck, I just cleaned it as best I could in my eight-year-old way. I did this a lot.

One day, when my mom was at the knit shop and my dad was doing a gig in Vegas, some of my brother's friends from the neigh-borhood who were six years older took me into a woodshed and did some inappropriate things to me. I honestly didn't understand what they were doing, but I always wanted to be accepted by the other kids, especially boys, so I went along with it. Afterward, my friend Sally told me that what they did was really wrong. So I talked to my mother. I told her that these boys took me into the woodshed and did something bad to me. Her response was typical of the time: "You just be quiet about that. Don't tell anyone about that. It's not nice." (She wanted to protect me, and this was obvi-ously long before the self-help and recovery movements.)

Well, I wasn't satisfied with that answer, so I wrote a letter to the boy's mother—or should I say the *perp*'s mother?—saying that if she didn't give me $10,000 by tomorrow, I was going to kill her. The next morning there were police cars surrounding the neighbors' house. Everyone was saying that this kid's mother had been threatened—$10,000 or her life. Who could it have been? Who could have threatened Mrs. Smith? Who was this dangerous extortionist with the handwriting of an eight-year-old? It was me, little Terry Ann Garr. I figured if my mother wasn't going to take care of this, I was.

Surprisingly, my extortion failed. But I was vindicated by the commotion I'd caused. No one would mess with me again . . . or so I thought.

Despite the fact that we didn't spend a whole lot of time together, my father knew I was dying to be in show business. I was already prancing around the living room like a little starlet. My father worked sporadically, depending on his health, doing bit parts on Red Skelton's show, *Our Miss Brooks,* and *I Love Lucy,* and even playing Marilyn Monroe's father in *Ladies of the Chorus.* Once, when he was on a show called *The Lone Wolf,* there was a part for a kid who was dying of cholera, and my father arranged for the role to go to my ten-year-old brother Phil. Needless to say, I was outraged. *I* was the one who was determined to be an entertainer, not Phil! I couldn't understand why Dad didn't get the part for me. What the hell was he thinking?

But being fair, or addressing his children's ambitions, wasn't a top priority for my dad. He had other business to attend to— like the Daily Doubles. He'd come home from the track having blown a month's worth of food money, and my mother would be furious. (Frank McCourt's family had nothing on us.) I'd hear the anger in her voice as she gave my father a piece of her mind, and I'd know exactly how to smooth things over. I would just make a funny face or laugh, ha-ha, about the money he'd lost until everything seemed all right again. At least until the next time. After the joy of gambling and drinking died down, the old "Irish melancholy" would set in, and I liked being able to make my dad happier, to be able to lighten his mood. I saw that, when I put my mind to it, I could have a real effect on the people around me. It felt good.

Soon I was staging elaborate shows in our garage. Tickets were collected; the audience, which included as many as six neighborhood kids, was ushered to their seats; an elaborate curtain my mother had sewn rose to reveal . . . me and my cohorts, tying up the curtain and squealing, "Don't look! Don't look!" For all the introductory rigmarole, the show itself might have been a bit anticlimactic. It generally consisted of a quick leap and a spin across the floor, a knock-knock joke or two, and many elaborate bows and curtsies. However amateurish, my song-and-dance routine became a more welcome distraction to me and to my mom as my dad's illness and gambling got worse.

Thank God he never let his addiction to the races get so out of hand that it interfered with his addiction to alcohol and cigarettes. (In those days, these habits were considered normal and cool, not like today, when they're just considered cool.) Years later, in 1988, after my father died, I did the movie *Let It Ride* with Richard Dreyfuss. We were filming at the Hialeah Racetrack in a suburb of Miami. When I called my mother to check in and told her where I was, she said, "Oh, do they have a statue of Daddy there?" Me: "Why?" Mom: "Well, your dad dumped so much money in that place, they should have some kind of memorial for him!" The truth is, the mention of any racetrack spurred my mother's anger, even twenty years later.

Maybe the reason my father gambled so much was that he was never satisfied with his showbiz success, or the lack thereof. He thought he had missed the boat, and said so. "Just when I got into vaudeville, it was dying," he'd say. "Then, when I got to Broadway, everyone went to L.A. to be in the movies, and then that was all over because of television, blah, blah, blah." He let the show-business life get to him. He could escape from his three kids and the ever-looming bills temporarily by having a few cocktails and blowing $500 on the fifth race at Santa Anita. But that feeling wouldn't last, and he didn't seem able to take responsibility for— or do anything about—what was happening in his life. Still, I would catch myself thinking, Maybe if he had stopped hanging out at the bar and the track long enough, he would have known where to catch the boat.

I was starting to understand what real responsibility was, and for that I can thank him. He was a good guy. He may not have been the perfect TV dad (this was before *The Simpsons*), but I loved my dad the best.

I could spend a lifetime in therapy trying to figure out my father, but the bottom line was that he was an Irish Catholic who liked to drink, gamble, and have fun. A typical comedian. But I shouldn't be too hard on him, so let me rephrase that: He was an *extremely funny and talented* Irish Catholic who liked to drink, gamble, and have fun. There, that's better.

Despite the pain, the lesson my father unwittingly taught me was that I couldn't rely on chance or fate if I wanted to succeed. I'd have to be completely dedicated to my career, independent, frugal in my spending, and sober in my choices (not just about booze). Furthermore, he didn't exactly make marriage look like an ideal to strive for. I sure as hell didn't want to depend on a man for my lifeline. Somewhere deep inside I thought, If this was what having a husband is like, who needs it? I'll just save my own little pennies and take care of myself.

By the time my father was in his early fifties, his lifestyle had begun to take a toll on his career and his health. The summer of 1955, my oldest brother, Ed, had just graduated from high school and was working for my cousin Hugh as a tour guide at the Grand Canyon. My mom, thirteen-year-old Phil, and I would drive there to see him on weekends. Dad had been sicker than usual that summer, so he stayed home. At the end of the summer we made a round-trip to the Grand Canyon to bring Ed home, and my dad stayed behind, as usual.

I will never forget the sound of my mother's voice when she went to tell my dad we were back. I was in my room and I heard her saying "Pappy! Pappy!" over and over. I can still remember her voice, getting louder and louder: "Pappy! Pappy!"

He never woke up.

My father's death was the saddest thing that had ever happened to me. It was unimaginably devastating, not just because I was eleven, but because my relationship with him was so unresolved. I was too young to realize how much I resented his vices and absences, too young to realize how much what we see, feel, and sense in our households and between our parents influences who we become. Or to appreciate how my mother defended my father and made excuses for him. She worshipped him, which is very different from love, and that imbalance would affect my love relationships with men for many years to come.

I *was* old enough to know that I had missed out on having a real

19

father who was interested in me, cared for me, supported me, and thought about me. I think I already knew I wanted to succeed where he had failed.

My father died thinking that he missed his boat. If he'd been around a little longer, I would have let him sail on mine.

3

Kwitcher Bitchin'

Losing a parent is a traumatic, life-changing experience for any kid. In two years, we had moved from a house I'd loved, and one of my parents was gone forever. Shrinks say I had a classic coping response—my survival instinct kicked in, and I knew what I had to do. I was going to fulfill my father's dream of being a famous performer. Since it hadn't happened for him, I was determined to make him proud.

I decided to become a prima ballerina, hopefully skipping the booze and the racetrack.

With my mother's blessing and hard-earned cash, I started taking three or four ballet classes a week. I practiced at home constantly. I danced every chance I got. Our living room wasn't huge, so the chairs and sofa became critical elements in my choreography. Somewhere in his travels, my father had acquired one of those high-tech NASA-endorsed contour chairs that tilted in all different directions for extreme comfort. That chair became my dance partner. (When it was down, I was up, and vice versa.) Nothing got in my way—there were no obstacles, only props. In fact, I owe the height of my leaps to that hideous chair.

Inevitably, my haphazard turns spun my brothers' homework off their laps. My miraculous leaps blocked their view of the TV. I was a pest. Or, as they so kindly put it, a brat, a crybaby, and a half A (by which they meant "half-ass," which I took as a compliment, since at least I wasn't a complete ass). Inevitably, they would throw things at me to interrupt my living-room solos. But what are a few pummelings when you're on your way to becoming a famous ballerina? I didn't care about anything but dancing. For the next three years, dance was my salvation. I lay awake at night practicing *tour jetés* in my head and obsessing about the ABT (American Ballet Theatre), imagining what I would look like in one of those sheer, flowing dresses Leslie Caron wore in *An American in Paris,* one of my favorite movies at the time.

By the time I started high school in beautiful downtown North Hollywood, I clearly remember having two lives. In school, I was self-conscious. My family wasn't like everyone else's. When my father died, my mother started working at NBC, making costumes, to support us. Most of the other kids' fathers supported their families as electricians or cameramen at the studios. When a classmate would say, "What do your mom and dad do for a living?" I'd answer that my mom made costumes and that my dad was dead . . . as a doornail. I could tell some of the kids felt sorry for me, so I kept to myself.

Even though I was fifteen, I was shy with the boys, too. Sure, I had mother-daughter talks all the time. We covered show business, agents, and eight-by-tens. But my mother never once mentioned boys or sex, not since she had shushed what happened to me in the woodshed when I was eight. Except once, when she was ironing. Out of the blue she turned to me with a dreamy look on her face and said, "You know, sex can be beautiful," and then went back to her ironing. I wasn't even sure she was talking to me.

So the first time a fifteen-year-old boy asked me on a date I had no idea what it was all about. This boy, Aaron, who lived down the block, asked me to go to a drive-in movie, *A Summer Place* with Troy Donahue. My mother and I both knew that Aaron's father had a Rambler, the front seat of which was a bench that reclined all the way back into a full-sized bed. Smartly, my mother vetoed the drive-in, suggesting a movie in the theater instead. I dutifully went back to Aaron and told him the rules. He said, "Here's what we do. You tell your mom we're going to a walk-in movie, and then we'll go to the drive-in instead."

"Hey, great idea," I said. "Why didn't I think of that?" I was curious about going on a date, and if lying was required for me to go, so be it.

When we got to the drive-in, Aaron immediately reclined the front seat and handed me a beer. I thought to myself, Here I am, fifteen, flat on my back, holding a Colt 45, which will spill if I try to take a sip. When Aaron kissed me I was less than thrilled. I barely knew him, and I wasn't the least bit attracted to him. It wasn't just that I was inexperienced; I actually didn't have much teenage curiosity. But, in concept at least, I liked the idea of having a boyfriend, and I didn't want to ruin my chances of seeing what all the fuss was about. So I went through the motions, but part of me already knew that this wasn't the kind of attention I wanted. It was almost too direct, like a bright light in my eyes. I was more at ease being admired from afar, much more comfortable in a dance class than I was being the object of a boy's affection, if that's what this was.

After school let out, my real life began. In this life, I wasn't self-conscious or confused in the least. I was a star in the making! I would hop on a bus, or sometimes two or three, to get to a dance class. I had watched Fred Astaire movies over and over again, and all I knew was that dancing felt as great as it looked. And I thought, it had something to do with sex. I loved the sensation of making my body do exactly what I told it to do. I liked the attention, being held up as an example for the rest of the class, being asked to demonstrate steps. (I was pretty good.) No matter what happened in school—with the other kids, with the classes that I couldn't stand—all was right at dance class: the smell of perspiration, the crunch of dipping my feet into boxes of rosin, toe shoes, classical piano music filling the air. It was the only thing that really fed me. It was another world.

The other dancers also became my world. We hung out in the dressing room, putting on our leotards and talking about boys and our hair and our bodies and how many pieces of celery we'd eaten that day. I had found my calling. It gave me an identity, a place where I could be myself and feel safe. It gave me a family.

After class I would meet my mom on the NBC lot in Burbank, as I'd been doing since junior high school. She was working in the costume department, making clothes for such stars as Gene Kelly, Frank Sinatra, Donald O'Connor, and Fred Astaire. Aside from the dance studio, that wardrobe stockroom became my home away from home. It was a young performer's fantasy. Basically, it was a huge warehouse filled with aisles and aisles of dresses, costumes, and other clothes that stars wore. The aisles were labeled NURSE, PRINCESS, LANA TURNER, DINAH SHORE, or ROSEMARY

CLOONEY. It was heaven—I carefully tried on whatever struck my fancy, then came out to the room where my mother, other women, and gay men (who weren't admitting they were gay because it was 19??) were sewing to show off my new look. I made believe I was Ginger Rogers dancing with Fred Astaire. I pretended I was cast to tap-dance with Gene Kelly and was late for my performance. I had to rush into costume and would run up and down the aisles in a pretend panic. Meeting stars like Rosemary Clooney and watching the goings-on of daily life backstage was endlessly thrilling until the novelty wore off and they just became like ordinary people who worked with my mom. Dance class was the dream, and being on the NBC lot made me feel like it could be a reality.

With my living-room dance performances and the four of us crunched in a tiny house, my older brother Ed—the academic among us—was desperate for a quiet place to study. My mother, with her usual makeshift genius, scavenged a used trailer from a yard sale with the idea of creating a place for Ed to study. The people having the yard sale weren't even trying to sell it, it was such a wreck. But my mom saw its infinite potential. Eyesore that it was, that trailer soon took up space in our little backyard, which was horrifying enough. But even worse was a sign on the back of the trailer that said, KWITCHER BITCHIN.' That sign! Being a typical teenager, I ordered my mother to take it down, but she refused. She was pleased with the new study, and with the way she'd managed to keep our lives together. She said, "No way. We're leaving that up to remind us not to complain."

In Kwitcher Bitchin' my mother found her perfect mantra, and eventually I was sold on it, too. Kwitcher Bitchin' kept me going when I was learning to dance. For all the pain and work, the bruises and the bloody toes, I knew that dancing made me happy, happier than I'd ever been. There was no way I was going to complain about anything.

I treated high school like an everyday chore, putting in the minimal effort required to get Bs and Cs and escape notice. Meanwhile, since dancing had become my life, I started trying to get paid to do it. The trade papers at my mom's job listed dance auditions, so I'd pore over them when visiting her, make a list of where and when they were, and finagle my way into any one I could, lying about my age.

One of my first roles was as a dancer in *Finian's Rainbow*. It was a semiprofessional Hollywood gig. I jumped around and rejoiced when I got the part, but part of me remained very calm. I was only sixteen, and I was already a girl on the move. In a sixteen-year-old-girl's way, I knew this was my destiny, and in some way I was always wholly confident that it would come to pass. For *Finian's Rainbow* I was just a chorus girl, dancing in the back, but I didn't care. There was a real wardrobe room, and I got to dress like an Irish villager, with a big peasant skirt and an apron. On the third night of the performance, one of the other dancers showed me that someone had written "f—k ye" in chalk on the stage. Every time I looked at the floor and saw "f—k ye," I would throw my head back and laugh heartily. I was a happy citizen of Loch Lomond (the little village in Finian's Rainbow), and I had just learned an early theatrical lesson: Incorporate all emotion, be it laughing or crying, into the scene you are doing.

I'd been taking buses all over the city—from school to dance class to auditions to NBC to home—for years. When I finally got my driver's license my mother bought a ten-year-old black and white Ford Fairlane for me to share with my brother Phil. Knowing my mother, it was some deal—finagled from a friend who was ditching it or whose aunt had died. I didn't ask for the details but thanked her profusely. That car changed my life. I quickly monopolized it, leaving the city buses behind, and drove to auditions all over the city.

This was okay with Phil. As long as I didn't drive the other car, the Volkswagen, he and Ed were happy. They claimed that I ground the gears on the Volkswagen, anyway. As for the Ford, it was huge—a real boat. It needed those big old tires on the side to dock it. The roads weren't wide enough for that car.

Like my mother, most performers lie about their age because they want to be younger. At my auditions I did the opposite: I pretended to be eighteen. I already had some practice at this. It had started a couple years earlier, when I was fourteen and hanging out in the costume department and one of the women from Donald O'Connor's variety show came in and offered me ten bucks to play her part. This involved standing in a doorway for two minutes. I was beside myself with joy. So there I was, sitting in the makeup chair for the first time, and the guy asked me what I wanted. I said, "I've got to look old. Really, really old."

"How old?" he asked.

And I said, "At least eighteen."

Once, during high school, I got offered a job in Las Vegas that included "mixing"—sitting down and having drinks with high rollers. My mother refused to let me go. Looking back, I can understand why she thought sending a teenage girl to get drunk with gamblers in Vegas was inappropriate. But at the time, I was outraged. I was an *artist*, and I needed to work! It took me forever to realize and recover from the fact that, at the time, a lot of people considered dancing one step above prostitution. They'd say "dancer/hooker" in the same breath. As you might imagine, I found this very upsetting. I mean, come on, you never heard "violinist/hooker"! But times change, and I'm sure it's different now. There's probably a violinist/hooker on every corner.

My ambition was now in full gear. I couldn't wait to finish high school because classes got in the way of my career. At the end of my senior year I auditioned for the cast of the Los Angeles Road Company production of *West Side Story*. The movie starring Natalie Wood, Richard Beymer, and Rita Moreno had just come out and was a raging success. Most of the dancers from the original Broadway cast and from the movie wanted to work in Hollywood, so they decided to be in the L.A. production to see if they could get some attention from the industry. As a result, the producers needed only to fill one or two spots in the supporting cast. So I went to a rehearsal hall somewhere in Hollywood with my friend Lynn and a bunch of other female dancers my age to try out for a part as one of the Jet girls.

I was eliminated right away. Didn't make it past the first round. Out. Finished. Good-bye.

I was crushed.

The dancing in the audition had been a breeze, but I guess my acting had hit the wrong note. I knew I was good enough for the part, so I stayed around and watched who they were choosing. It seemed to be nonsmiling tough chicks . . . I could do that. Then my friend Lynn told me she'd been called back. The second round of auditions was the next day. Perfect! I said to Lynn, "I'm going with you." Lynn said, "Teri, you were dinged. You can't go back!" To which I brazenly replied, "They'll never remember me. Besides, I know what they want now." I was convinced that they didn't choose me because I smiled too much. So I went to the callback, and I was cast as a Jet girl. And Lynn, despite her legitimate callback, wasn't. Apparently, that's showbiz. I don't think she ever forgave me for that.

When it came to my burgeoning career, I wasn't going to accept rejection. If they didn't realize how great I was, I had to give them a little "nudge." For their own good, of course.

4

My Affair with Mickey Mouse

The leap from *West Side Story* to the Oscars didn't feel anything like the soaring, weightless leaps I learned in ballet. It was more like a long, trafficky road riddled with speedbumps. When I defiantly went to the callbacks for *West Side Story*, my stubbornness was rewarded. I got the part of Velma, a Jet girl. I graduated from high school on a Friday, and on Saturday I started rehearsals. I had one measly line in the musical, but it was my first measly line ever, and I was very excited about it.

The line was "No, thank *you*, ooo, ooo, ooo-blio!"

No, I don't know what "ooo-blio" meant, either. No one did. I think it was supposed to be hip and jazzy. It was written by Arthur Laurents, so I was sure it was kosher, plus it always got a laugh. Thanks to that one line, I considered myself at the tender age of ?? not just a professional dancer, but also a professional actress and comedienne. (Hello, Mr. Slifkin, I'm cooking now.) This was progress! But it didn't take long for me to notice that another dancer had a better line. She got to say, "I and Velma ain't dumb." As far as I was concerned, that line was the best, and I wanted it to be mine.

Rather than pull a Tonya Harding–style kneecapping on my rival, I accepted my fate. Some of my early ballet classes had taught me more than how to execute leaps and turns. Back in junior high school, when my mother was working on *The Dinah Shore Show,* I met Dinah Shore's daughter, Melissa, who was taking a dance class in Beverly Hills. Her teacher was a brilliant Russian, David Lichine, who had danced and choreographed throughout the world. In my mind, anything Dinah Shore did or said was perfect. It was clear to me that if I was going to be the best, I had to go there. I was adamant. I don't know how my mother paid for the classes with David Lichine, but somehow she managed to do it, and David Lichine taught me how to be a resilient professional.

It took over an hour on four different buses for me to get from the Valley to Beverly Hills for David Lichine's classes (remember, I'm in junior high here, so it's pre–Ford Fairlane). Unfazed, I did all my homework on the bus, making sure I kept up with my schoolwork so nothing would interfere with my dancing. The long trip was worth every second.

The class was full of rich Beverly Hills kids whose moms would drop them off and pick them up. One slightly older student, Kris Harmon, was dating Ricky Nelson at the time. (She'd later marry him and play his wife on *Ozzie and Harriet*.) In the dressing room, she would talk about how cute he was. I was like any other starstruck kid. I'd ask her everything about him and then, when she answered, all I could think was, Oh my God, she's talking about Ricky Nelson! Oh my God, Ricky Nelson! Half the time, I didn't pay attention to what she actually said about him, so then I'd ask all over again. I was in love with him, too. Wasn't everybody?

And there you have it, my career in a nutshell: focused on my work, but starstruck and groupie-fied whenever a cute boy was mentioned.

I may have been a blathering idiot, but David Lichine was the real thing. A Russian dancer. And his wife, who assisted in class, was even more Russian, right down to her name: Tatiana Riabouchinska. Tatiana and David had come to America with nothing but their thick Russian accents to dance and to teach after being with the Ballet Russe de Monte Carlo and Ballet Theatre (now ABT). Their studio was above a candy store on Beverly Drive in the heart of Beverly Hills. It was the usual couple of wood-floored, mirrored rooms, but it was different from any other classroom I had ever been in.

I studied with David all the way through high school. He taught me dance lessons that became life lessons. One time, when I was in ninth grade, our class had its annual recital. All the parents were watching, and I had to do a *grande jeté*. (This is when you run across the stage and jump with your legs splayed in opposite directions.) Since I was all about being a star, even at fourteen, I kicked out my legs in a real show-off move. David walked over to me and said quickly, so the others would hear, "Terry, an artist doesn't call attention to herself. You need to have technique to express your art. That does not include showing off," thereby embarrassing me. Humbled, I took his advice to heart. I learned that you can still express yourself working within limits, that sometimes that's even more compelling than going over the top. By the time I got to say my line as a Jet girl, I was ready to do it.

Every now and again, during rehearsals for *West Side Story*, I would notice that my right foot felt strange. It didn't hurt, exactly; it just got a little tingly. For as long as I could remember, my left leg had always been stronger than my right leg, and I'd thought of it as a quirky asset. Now I was seventeen and the difference was more pronounced, but David Lichine's voice again resonated in my head. I knew what he would say: "You fall down, you get up! We all make mistakes. You just keep going." Plus, I was trained to handle discrepancies between my body and my mind. Dancers take pride in aching feet and muscles, and I wasn't about to complain about some funny tingle. Besides, I had David Lichine on a loop in my head, saying: "You fall down, you get up!" If you knew how many times David Lichine has repeated this in my head throughout my life, it would astound you. In fact, I hear him right now. You know, I wish he would shut up already.

I was in *West Side Story* for six weeks, which earned me my Actor's Equity card. Getting in the union was a big deal; it meant I was legit. I took my $100 a week and literally stuffed it under my mattress until I had enough to buy a stereo so that I could practice to music in my room. I was doing the work I loved, getting dancing parts, and actually getting paid. I thought I had died and gone to heaven.

My mother and my aunt Alice came to the opening night of *West Side Story* at the Moulin Rouge Theater in Hollywood. Twenty years earlier that particular theater had been a burlesque club called Earl Carroll's where both my parents had worked. My poor mother must have been caught between nostalgia for their early days and pride for her daughter. She and my brothers sent me a telegram that said, FILL THE SHOES!—like I wasn't feeling enough pressure already! But that telegram made me happy because it would have made my dad proud. Assuming it was his shoes they were talking about.

Being in *West Side Story* changed my life. During the musical I had a revelation. By reputation, Jerome Robbins was really the first choreographer to make dancers think and act. In other shows I watched some of the dancers try to act, and thought that all they did was scrunch up their faces like they smelled something bad. I wanted to do better than that—to dance like I smelled something good, at the very least. Luckily, Tony Mordente, who was married to Chita Rivera at the time, directed the show. Between Robbins's choreography and Mordente's direction, we were encouraged to do more than just go through the moves. Tony was always talking about the legendary Actors Studio and how the group theater had influenced Jerry Robbins. The more I contemplated my reasons for dancing, the more I realized movement wasn't the only way for me to express myself. It began to dawn on me that I wanted not just to dance, but to act (especially after getting laughs from the "ooo-ooo-blio" line).

After *West Side Story* closed, the actor who played Baby John, David Winters, started a dance class in West Hollywood. I was totally in love with him, so naturally I would go down there every day to dance. (I guess I wasn't his type since he later married porn star Linda Lovelace.) I was in his class with my longtime friend Toni Basil who I had met when we both danced in *West Side Story*. I was still living with my mother in the Valley, but Toni already had her very own apartment in Hollywood. Boy, did I envy her! Toni grew up in a show-business family in Las Vegas. Her father was the band leader at the Sahara in Vegas. She was already working, dancing in a cage at the Billionaires' Club. At her apartment she had false eyelashes, hairpieces, and a waist cincher. This level of accessorizing impressed me. As far as I was concerned, it made Toni a real show-business dancer. I was in awe of her. She was everything I wanted to be. Toni would end up a successful dancer, choreographer, musician, and actress, releasing the worldwide hit song "Mickey." She was my partner in crime then, as she is now.

Toni and I worked very hard in David Winters's class. Ann-Margret was in the class, too. When she got the lead in an Elvis movie, she asked David to be the choreographer, and he accepted. I will never forget the day he entered our class in March 1963 and announced, "Okay, I'm choreographing an Elvis movie, so I want you all to come over to MGM next week and audition."

Elvis was a big deal to me. Okay, he was a big deal to everyone, but I felt that I had a very special connection to him. One summer in high school I had made it into the Ballet Celeste, a summer dance company out of San Francisco. The woman who ran the company was from the Ballet Russe (like David Lichine and his wife), and it was hard-core. We lived and breathed ballet. We walked like ducks all the time, with our feet turned out in first position. Dropping a napkin was an excuse for a plié. My hair was in a permanent bun. We spent the first part of the summer in the company boardinghouse, where they monitored what we ate, what we read, and what music we heard. For the first few weeks, we practiced all day long. Then we packed up a bus and took the ballet on tour across the country. This was what I had dreamed about. I had wanted to be in the American Ballet Theatre, and this was the first step.

As the summer passed, however, the intensity became a little much for me. Everyone was so serious all the time. In Seattle, one of the tour stops, I had the brilliant idea to toss water bombs out the window of the hotel, just to break up the day. Then, out of the blue, I heard an Elvis Presley song wafting through the open window. It was "Hard Headed Woman." I thought, Hey, there's something going on out there, and I want to know what it is. It was the first nonclassical music I'd heard all summer, and when I came home from the tour, with a taste of soul music and rhythm and blues, I didn't want to focus solely on ballet. I started studying other kinds of dance. Suddenly, ballet seemed uptight, and when I saw the dancers in movies like *Seven Brides for Seven Brothers,* I wanted to move like them instead. (Later I realized that without the foundation of ballet, you *can't* dance like that.)

Years later, the Elvis movie that Ann-Margret was starring in was called *Viva Las Vegas.* I auditioned and got the role of a chorus-line dancer. This fit right into my master plan. I was on my way (even though I didn't know what direction I was headed).

Toni was David's assistant, so I was privy to all the behind-the-scenes scoop on the movie. The gossip was that Ann-Margret, the big star, was taught all the dances in the back, beforehand, so that when she came out to learn the steps with the rest of the dancers, she'd already be good. I had already been training for ten years as a dancer, and all the others languishing in the chorus line were equally talented. And yet we would sit on a bench between scenes, smoking cigarettes and drinking tap water, while each of the stars had a trailer and twenty-five people tending to her every need. The stars had shrimp cocktails ordered in. We were lucky if they offered us gum. The stars had several changes of costumes custom-made and delivered clean every day. We wore our own clothes, took them home to wash them, and put them on again the next day. And we were working at least as hard as the stars, and were just as (or more) talented.

I thought, What gives? What is the secret formula for getting from this cold, hard bench to that comfy trailer? I didn't get it. Learning the nature of the business fueled my drive. I didn't think this was fair, exactly. I wasn't against working hard, but I wanted to be in front. And the shrimp cocktail—I wanted that, too.

Chorus line or not, being in an Elvis movie was pretty cool. It still is cool—especially to those who persist in hailing him as the King, myself included. Elvis's entourage, "The Memphis Mafia," as they were known, were great guys. They were all his old friends from growing up in Memphis; he took care of his own. Over the course of dancing in a number of his movies (including *Roustabout*, *Kissin' Cousins*, *Speedway*, and *Clambake*), I got to know Elvis and his Memphis Mafia. They were all gentlemanly. It just happened that Elvis was the famous and talented one.

One night, it happened to be Good Friday, when I was still living with my mom in the Valley, the shooting ran late on the set of *Viva Las Vegas*, as it often did on Friday nights. This particular night one of his boys said, "You wanna go to a party at Elvis's house?" We all said, "Okay, sure!" I rode with my girlfriend Carrie to this alleged "party" at the house Elvis had rented in Bel Air. After the long ride to the rented mansion, we walked in to find that there was no party. No chips, no dips, just Elvis, his boys, and a couple of girls sitting around. They should have just said, "Come on up and we can all watch Elvis watch TV and play pool." There was no alcohol, but there were cases of Coca-Cola. So there we sat, watching Elvis and drinking Coke.

It got later and later, until finally my friend Carrie, who had been flirting with Elvis, wound up disappearing into the bedroom with him. Just so you know, she swore they didn't "do it." Knowing Carrie, it's the truth. Whatever went on in that room, I was stuck waiting for what felt like forever for my ride home. Pretty soon everyone else was gone. I didn't know what to do. I couldn't interrupt them; it was Elvis, for the love of God! So I waited, all alone on the couch, until it started to get light outside. I looked at my watch. It wasn't Good Friday anymore. It was 6 A.M. on Holy Saturday. I was usually such a Girl Scout. All I could think was, My mother is going to kill me. I started running through the litany of possible excuses. If I said, "I spent the night at so-and-so's house," she'd say, "Oh, I called there. I called the hospitals, too."

Finally, at seven o'clock, Carrie came out of the bedroom, closing the door quietly behind her. I guess Elvis was still asleep. Of course, I wanted to hear every detail of her adventure, but I was distracted by my impending doom. I shouted, "I'm going to kill you! I'm gonna have to lie to my mother! I have to think up a story, and a good one, fast!" I was a wreck the whole drive back to my mother's house in Van Nuys, but part of me actually believed that the truth—the "I was at a party at Elvis Presley's house" excuse—might work. Now that I have my own daughter, I see how awful the waiting must have been for her, but at the time it seemed reasonable.

I quietly opened the front door. Mom was sitting on the couch, in her pajamas, with her arms folded across her chest. The bags under her eyes told me she hadn't slept all night. I said, "Oh no, you're up, I'm really sorry we're so late, I mean early. We went to this party. Ma, it was at Elvis Presley's house. I mean, everyone was having such a good time, we just didn't realize what time it was, and we just stayed and gosh, I just looked out the window and it was light, and I couldn't believe how late it was, and we rushed right home!" My mother sat quietly and listened to the story before she looked me directly in the eye and said, "Jesus Christ is dying on the cross, and you are at Elvis Presley's!"

Mom was always more of a Bing Crosby fan.

I ended up dancing in nine Elvis movies. When he was working on a movie, away from his Tennessee home, he was a fish out of water. His real love was performing live in front of an audience. As much as the dancers and cast members adored him, we couldn't replace the thrill of thousands of fans screaming his name. Once, in the middle of filming *Clambake*, he told me, "I'll do whatever they tell me. If we were making a record, I'd have something to say, but this is a movie, and I'll just do as I'm told." He was sweet, always saying, "Yes, sir," and "No, ma'am," like a kid out of military school. He was just so polite. He had more natural charisma in his pinkie than all the producers of his movies combined.

Right around the time when I was dancing in Elvis's movies, my brother Ed was taking a more traditional route. He'd married a lovely girl from high school named Bunny Hanzi in 1962. It was a big Catholic wedding in a church. I was a bridesmaid, wearing a puke green dress and a matching hat with a net veil. I looked like an exterminator. The only thing missing was a tank of insecticide strapped to my back. I thought Bunny looked beautiful, and I was happy for them, but I didn't have the whole white-wedding fantasy. My nephew, Danny, was born two years later, in 1964. And then my niece, Lisa, was born just seventeen months after Danny. In quick order Ed, a Vietnam vet, had become a doctor, a husband, and a father, with a regular family life out in the Valley, complete with home-cooked meals, a lawn mower, and a two-car garage. He experienced an entire life cycle in the period of time I spent looking for a really cute date.

I loved my new nephew and niece and went over the hill to visit them all the time. It was an escape from my crazy life and the nut-jobs I hung out with. (And as a bonus, this made the phrase *over the hill* a lot more palatable.) Bunny made Martha Stewart look like an underachiever, with her centerpieces and perfect decor. Part of me saw the appeal of that homemaker world, but I decided that I wanted to play house more than I wanted to clean house. I adored those kids, but the reality of raising a family wasn't on my mind. There was something appealing about it, but the family tableau hadn't exactly panned out for me so far. I had found other ways to drive myself crazy.

In between Elvis movies I took assorted other jobs. I did a lot of backer's auditions for my friend Larry Billman, who once wrote a musical about *Ripley's Believe It or Not*. One of the songs contained the operatic lyric "In Colorado there is a cow, with two udders, one on her back." Not exactly *Madame Butterfly*.

Another time he wrote a show called *Show Me America* that was to be performed at Disneyland. He asked if I wanted to play the Statue of Liberty on roller skates. Roller skates? No problem! I'd roller-skated as a kid.

We couldn't rehearse onstage because the park was always open, so opening night was our first performance. My entrance was during the "You're a Grand Old Flag" number. I was supposed to skate down from the top of a ramp to the edge of the stage while Ping-Pong balls and confetti shot out of my torch.

As I skated down the ramp with those big skates on, I started going faster and faster. I looked around at my fellow players for help. They just kept dancing and smiling. I dragged my toe stop and just started skidding down the ramp; it didn't stop me at all. Finally, I just skated off the end of the stage and flew into the orchestra pit, landing on top of John Scott Trotter, the bandleader.

We were all wearing body mics, and mine was taped right in the middle of my chest. Someone came and tried to haul me out of the pit. Thinking I was whispering, I said, "Let go of me, you asshole, you're not helping!" Lots more swearing ensued. "Son of a bitch, bastard, I'm fine, damn it!" Every time I put my skate on the stage it would slip out from under me and I'd fall on my butt again.

All the while, all this "shit, damn, hell" stuff was, of course, booming out of my microphone and echoing off the Matterhorn.

I was sure Walt Disney was turning over in his grave. In fact, I felt like any second he was going to tap me on the shoulder and say, "You're fired!"

This was during the early '60s, and the Warren Commission had just declared that there was no conspiracy to assassinate President Kennedy. Society had bigger threats to worry about, apparently—like the possibility of a skating Statue of Liberty being a communist. In those days, if you wanted to work at Disneyland you had to sign a paper that said you weren't a communist. Believe me, I would have signed a paper saying I was Zoroastrian. But I used to smuggle friends into Disneyland in the trunk of my car so they didn't have to pay the entrance fee. That was my big "up-yours" to Disneyland for violating my rights as an American.

Over in Frontierland there was a Western Show starring a guy named Wally Boag. He did a bit where another guy would hit him in the jaw and white beans would fly out of his mouth to look like teeth. Around this time Steve Martin was selling popcorn in front of the Saloon. He learned Wally's act backward and forward and also made balloon animals and performed magic tricks. (See, everyone has to start somewhere.) At the time, Steve was nobody, just like me, and now he's "Steve Martin of *The New Yorker*" and I'm . . . well, I'm not at Disneyland anymore.

I didn't really know Steve then, but he and I would become friends a few years later. After skating as the Statue of Liberty for eight hours Monday through Friday, I wasn't much for socializing. All that liberty and justice can be exhausting.

5

Buried Alive

When my stint at Disneyland was over, I decided to pay a visit to Lady Liberty herself. I wanted to try my luck in New York City. My mother had told me about a place called the Rehearsal Club, which was the setting of the classic play and movie *Stage Door* with Katharine Hepburn and Ginger Rogers. The Rehearsal Club was a theatrical boardinghouse for girls in a big brownstone on Fifty-third Street, right down the block from the Museum of Modern Art. It was founded in 1913 by Jane Harris Hall and Jean Greer Robinson, two women who had taken an interest in improving the lot of young actresses in Manhattan, and was something of a presence until it finally closed in 1980.

There was a parlor where we were allowed to bring "gentleman callers," but absolutely no men were allowed past there, an anachronism even in those days. An aging Broadway diva named Estelle ran the place. She spoke with a fake British accent and thought she was Joan Crawford.

Two kinds of girls lived at the Rehearsal Club. There were rich Connecticut debutante girls who wanted to be actresses, and poor dancer girls who had come to New York to seek their fortunes. I was part of the latter group, and I was allowed to stay there because my mother had been a Rockette. For once I was grateful for my vaudeville legacy. But I have to say, I lived in a converted closet—not the best room in the place. I paid $25 a week for room and board. There was a cafeteria in the basement where we were given two meals a day, breakfast and dinner. If we didn't show up at both meals in a neat skirt and conservative sweater, we'd get fierce scowls from not–Joan Crawford. The rich girls used to order in from the Stage Deli. They would get pastrami sandwiches with Russian dressing. I shared them sometimes and thought, This is the best food I have ever eaten; I'd better figure out a way to make money so I can afford these delicious pastrami sandwiches myself.

I was determined to master Manhattan in my attempt to validate my résumé with some real theatrical credits. So I sat down to study a map. Fifth, Madison, Park, Lex, Third, Second, and on and on and on. Cake. Now the east-west streets—Fifty-third, Fifty-fourth, Fifty-fifth, Fifty-sixth—okay, I've detected a pattern here, too. Years later, I would get to know these streets like the back of my hand, each freckle a doctor's office. But at that time, my only tasks were to orient myself, find a theater agent, rustle up some friends to hang out with, and start auditioning whenever and wherever I could.

In the basement of the Rehearsal Club, there was a bulletin board that posted the latest auditions. An old hand at auditions, I started going out on them right away. But these were harder than I expected, and different from those in Hollywood. Michael Kidd, who was famous for having choreographed *Seven Brides for Seven*

Brothers, Guys and Dolls, and many other Broadway musicals, was casting *Ben Franklin in Paris,* a Broadway musical about Ben Franklin arriving in Paris in search of support for the Colonies' war against the British. The audition consisted of difficult routines, and there were hundreds of girls there. We all lined up along Shubert Alley in the Broadway district and were given numbers. I was number 143. In Hollywood, when I auditioned for movies or TV, sometimes all I had to do was shake my butt. In these Broadway auditions, however, I had to be focused, in perfect shape, ready to work out, and able to perform the new combinations with impeccable timing from the get-go.

The callback narrowed the field down to twenty-five girls, and I was one of them. I entered with confidence. After all, I had my ballet background. Michael Kidd leaned against the wall. He was short and dark-haired, with a dancer's physique, and he wore fitted black pants. His sleeves were rolled high to display lean, muscular arms. He looked exactly as I thought a Broadway choreographer should. This was the real thing. I was going to be a Broadway dancer!

Michael taught us a short, difficult ballet combination using every element of dance: jumps, leaps, pirouettes, fortes. We ran through the routine for about fifteen minutes. After the third or fourth take, he said, "Okay, everybody stop and line up onstage." There was silence. Michael said, "Who tripped on that *grande jeté?*" He asked so casually that I thought he was going to give me a tip on how to do the step, so I raised my hand. He said, "Thank you very much, good-bye." Wow. That was it! One strike and I was out. That sobered me up. In Hollywood, if I didn't shake my butt right the first time, I got another chance. But now I was in the Big Apple, and there were no second chances.

Needless to say, that was the last time I admitted to making a mistake. New York City. The year was 1964.

That first attempt to make it in New York quickly wore thin. The jobs weren't exactly rolling in, so I was always broke and wondering where my next pastrami sandwich was coming from. I was barely making my rent when I got a call from my old friend and teacher David Winters. He offered me a job dancing in an NBC special with the Supremes. And I wouldn't even have to audition! In a flash, I scraped together the money for a plane ticket, packed my one big suitcase, and it was back to Hollywood for me. I'd only been in New York a few months when I bid the city farewell. I had no idea I'd be back and forth for the rest of my life.

When I returned to L.A., my mother insisted that I go to college. She and my father had never gone, and a college education was her idea of how her kids would live better lives. I wanted none of it,* so I decided the best thing to do would be to move out of her house. But before I could find myself an apartment, my mom got her way. Somehow, before I knew it, I was enrolled at Cal State Northridge, in the speech/drama department. At least I'd be able to do theater—or so I thought. I remember auditioning for plays like *Agamemnon,* and they'd say, "Very good, would you like to build sets in the shop?" And I'd think, Hey, I'm a professional! I have union cards! I watched Elvis drink Coke!

At Cal State I took all the required courses, like German, anthropology, and biology. They were impossible. Between classes, I would go to the cafeteria and sit with the girls who were getting all the parts in the college plays. I thought they were my people, but

---

*Note to my daughter and other impressionable youth: A good education is very important. Stay in school!

instead of discussing roles and auditions, they would talk about coffeepots, Crock-Pots, and the crackpot they were going to marry. In those days, a lot of women went to college for an MRS. degree and made no pretense of wanting an education. At least, that was the case with the ones I encountered. It may have been the late '60s, but these gals were freeze-dried in the '50s.

I tried to have patience with the German classes and the set-building, but I was really only interested in auditions. One of my showbiz uncles was Ben Wrigley. For years I thought he was my real uncle. Then I figured out that he was just a dog-act pal of my dad's from Philly who was trying to make his way in Hollywood. He'd perform at bar mitzvahs, charity events, community fund-raisers—anywhere someone might see him and give him his big break. He did manage to get on Ed Sullivan's show once, but it never amounted to much. Uncle Ben *did* hook me up with his agent, Coralie Jr., who had her own agency called (guess what?) the Coralie Jr. Theatrical Agency. She handled mostly specialty acts, little people and strippers and eccentric dancers like Ben. She wasn't the most high-powered agent, but I was glad to have her. Any agent was better than no agent. Every Friday I would buy the trades to see the TV production charts. Then I'd call up Coralie and say, "*Room 222* needs three students. I can be a student. Send them my picture!" Once I did a few shows like *Room 222* and *Dr. Kildare,* the casting agents knew me and started calling Coralie to invite me back for more.

Then I struck gold. I used my TV credits to land a commercial agent, who got me an ad for Crest toothpaste. Next thing I knew I was doing masses of commercials: Safeguard soap, First National Bank, Greyhound bus line, Camay, Bold detergent, Datsun, Nationwide Insurance, Sure deodorant, General Foods breakfast squares, Joy, Chevrolet, Doritos, Cheer, Glad, and on and on. I was the all-American girl next door (actually, the girl next door to the girl next door), and it seemed like all I had to do in commercial auditions was hold a product up next to my face, smile, and say, "Buy this!" and I'd get the job. Nobody seemed to figure out that an endorsement from me didn't say anything about the product. The good news was, in those days, every time they showed the commercial, they had to pay me a residual. So I was finally making a living, and a good one.

So much for college. One day in the cafeteria, as I listened to the MRS. candidates who were getting all the parts in the plays drone on, I decided I'd had enough. The double life of student and starlet wasn't worth it. Even my mother had to admit that I was doing pretty well. Besides, we figured I could go back to finish college whenever I wanted. Maybe later—like never. I headed back to Hollywood full-time.

I was still living at home with my mother, but I needed a change. She was too heavily invested in my career. Every day she wanted to hear the minute details of my meeting with a casting agent or what I'd read in my auditions. She was obviously proud of me, and her curiosity was harmless, so it was hard to complain, but I felt I was getting too old to give my mother a daily report. She was kind of living through me, and it was starting to get on my nerves.

So I told her I wanted to move out. She was absolutely against it. She told me it was a waste of money, and possibly dangerous for a young, innocent girl like me. But I think she was grasping for excuses. She just didn't want me to go.

I proceeded to look for an apartment with my friend Carrie— the same Carrie who'd had the Good Friday flirtation with Elvis.

(Her Ouija board was still telling her that Elvis would ask her to marry him, but, alas, it wasn't to be.) She was friends with Frank Sinatra's nephew Richard, who told us that the apartment next to his, a dumpy little two-bedroom on Gower in a busy section of Hollywood, was available. The apartment was in an old Spanish-style building and had cracked tile floors and a crappy balcony overlooking an intersection that was shrouded in exhaust. But we were excited that it was ours, and we couldn't wait to move in.

Carrie took the bedroom and I slept on a pullout couch in the living room. At first I didn't tell my mother that I'd rented an apartment. I just let her think I spent the night on the couch at my girlfriend's apartment. (Which, come to think of it, is kind of what I did, but for a fee.) By the time my mom caught on, it was a done deal.

I loved having my own apartment. For so long I'd wanted to set up house, and I finally got to. I put cheap curtains on the windows and filled the window boxes with flowers. I sang in the shower and danced in the living room. So what if the heater was broken and there was no electricity in the bathroom? It was mine. I was living my fantasy of being a sophisticated career girl, not unlike Toni Basil herself. Soon after, I started taking an acting class taught by one of the legendary acting teachers, Eric Morris. Among the students in my class were my old friend Toni Basil, Harry Dean Stanton, Maggie Blye, and Jack Nicholson, among others.

In those days, Jack Nicholson was more of a writer than an actor. He wrote a psychedelic film called *Head* as a vehicle for the Monkees. It was a plotless musical journey to nowhere. The good news was that when Jack wrote it, he included parts for all the girls in our class. I even had a line of dialogue. A rattlesnake bit me on the finger, and I had to say to Mickey Dolenz, "Suck it, before the venom reaches my heart!" Sounds just like Jack, right? Even though it was just one line, it was three words longer than "I and Velma ain't dumb," so it was a step in the right direction. Shortly after *Head* was released, Jack appeared in *Easy Rider,* and the rest is history.

After class, we'd all go out drinking, and I soon started dating the most handsome boy in the class. He had the aristocratic name Hampton Fancher III, but we called him Handsome Grandstand. He was very dashing—tall, dark, and, of course, handsome—and he was older than I. He'd already been married, briefly, to Sue Lyon, who played the title role in Stanley Kubrick's *Lolita.* Hampton was my first real love (and not only because when we went to visit his family I could tell my friends we were going to the Hamptons' for the weekend). He was fun and smart, chivalrous and talented.

We'd only been dating for a couple months when we ran into a guy who owed me money. His name was Fred, and I'd dated him briefly just after college. He'd bought my old car but had never finished paying me for it. Hampton, knight in shining armor that he was, leapt to defend my honor—or my fifty dollars. What a guy. He'd been working on a construction crew (for "material"— he wanted to be a writer), and he was pretty tough. The two of them went at it until the cops showed up and carted Hampton away. I was horrified, but when I went to bail him out, Hampton said, "No, leave me here. This is great." He thought being in jail was good material. And who knows, maybe he sat in that cell and imagined: I am Blade Runner, a policeman of the future specializing in the termination of replicants. Because nearly twenty years later Handsome Grandstand would write the movie *Blade Runner.* See how things happen?

One of the guys who hung out with us was Dennis Hopper. At the time he was an actor, photographer, art collector, and bon vivant. We became friendly; he introduced me to a lot of people from the art world: Ed Ruscha, Billy Al Bengston, Wallace Berman, Joe Goode, Robert Graham, and many others. They were the demimonde of the Southern California art scene. We'd do poetry readings on the Santa Monica pier in a lofty space up above the merry-go-round. I'd read poems that Michael McClure wrote. (He'd later write the iconic '60s play *The Beard,* in which Jean Harlow and Billy the Kid meet in eternity.) This was my escape from showbiz—hanging out with this totally cool group of Venice beat artists and contemplating the meaning of life.

That whole group was reckless, and Dennis was the ringleader. He took me and Toni to love-ins and peace marches, and he was the only guy I knew who had the guts to drive his Corvair convertible (with the top down!) through a wall of flames during the Watts Riots. He may have been stoned at the time (who wasn't), but at least the rioters didn't stone him. I remember watching the riots from a safer haven, sitting in a restaurant with Wallace Berman and Hampton on Sunset Boulevard, up above the city. We watched the smoke billowing up from downtown L.A. I said to Wallace, "This is terrible. What's going to happen?" He just shook his head and said, "You can't put people in ghettos."

Hampton and I dated for nearly a year, and then we broke up. To this day he insists that I was the one who wanted out, but when I remember how dashing he was, it's hard to believe. I know that I regretted the breakup, but I never admitted it, not to myself or to my friends. I was like a horse with blinders on—so determined to run the race that I didn't pay any attention to what might have been happening on the sidelines.

When it ended I was still living in the apartment on Gower Street. My roommate Carrie had moved out, and one of my oldest friends from junior high school, Fran, moved in. Fran had been the prettiest girl in my high school. She was tall, with high cheekbones and long, thick, dark brown hair—a Cindy Crawford type. Even years later, at our twenty-fifth high-school reunion (which she didn't attend), the men got moony just remembering her.

When Hampton and I broke up, someone told me that he'd started dating Fran. I didn't believe it. Fran had witnessed our whole relationship. And besides, she and I were old, loyal friends. But one day I was driving down Gower Street and I saw Hampton driving in the other direction in his forest green Morris Minor. Sitting beside him in the passenger seat was none other than Fran!

I was so upset that I had to pull over to the side of the road. I went home and paced the apartment until Fran showed up. When I confronted her, all she said was, "But you were done with him. It was over." She just didn't get it. So much for female solidarity. It stunned me at the time, but looking back, I'm sure it had to do with some classic Freudian father-mother thing. Doesn't everything come back to a Freudian father-mother thing?

I thought about the situation for about half a second. Here was my friend, late with her rent, borrowing my clothes without asking, and sleeping with my ex-boyfriend. The betrayal was the last straw. I kicked her out of the apartment and never spoke to her again. No one got away with that with Terry Ann Garr! Now it just seems like petty, childish angst, but at the time it was big.

And Fran . . . She always wanted to be a model, but ended up a checkout girl at Von's. Or so I like to tell myself.

Near the end of that year Toni Basil told me that she had gotten a job on a Princess Grace special. They wanted dancers to perform in the palace in Monaco. Post-breakup, I needed to clear my head. Besides, I was feeling flush from all the commercial work I'd gotten, and I'd never gone on a real vacation with friends, so I decided to take the job. My friend Ann Marshall was going with us. On the way to the south of France, we decided to do a stopover in London! Groovy, baby!

It turned out that Ann had mentioned our plans to a friend, Steve, who was the road manager for the Mamas and Papas. He told us that Cass Elliott (a Mama) had an apartment in London that she wouldn't be using, so he'd be staying there and we could, too.

It was the height of the Beatles craze, and Toni, Ann, and I were going to be in London while they were there. We went around London saying, "Maybe we'll run into them." In London we connected with the art crowd. We thought about doing basic tourist stuff, like going to see Buckingham Palace and the Tower of London, but mostly we went to art galleries, museums, and snooty private nightclubs the likes of which I'd never seen before. A few days before we were scheduled to leave, Steve, the road manager, came in and said, "How would you girls like to go to a Beatles recording session?" You never saw three girls move so fast in your life.

At the studio we listened to them record "Yellow Submarine." We sat on plastic chairs outside the sound room and stared at them through a glass window. I thought I smelled pot. I sat on my hands so I wouldn't clap and bit my lip so I wouldn't squeal like any girl my age would have felt compelled to do. I couldn't believe my luck. They sang "Yellow Submarine" straight through five times, and it sounded perfect to me every single time. Dancing in Elvis films had been great, but this was surreal. Toni, Ann, and I were literally pinching each other.

After the Beatles were finished, Steve introduced us to John Lennon. He was lovely, and gentle, and showed us his new car, a Rolls-Royce painted like a gypsy caravan, with brightly colored flowers all over it. He said, "You birds want to go out for a ride?" Did we ever! So the three of us climbed into the car with all four Beatles and Steve, and we went to a nightclub. We drank wine and danced, then went to another club, where we drank more wine and danced some more. It went on like that all night.

As it started to get light out, John said, "Let's go to my house." It was eight in the morning. His wife Cynthia was there, and their son, Julian, was riding around on his tricycle. They seemed completely unfazed by the fact that John was coming home at daybreak with a bunch of American rock-and-roll groupies. Eventually, we went home, but we saw them throughout the rest of our stay in London. The doorbell at our flat would ring, we'd look out the second-story window, and there would be George Harrison, wanting to know if anyone was home. (Of course, it's possible that they were more interested in seeing Steve than us. Steve kept some sort of chemistry set on the coffee table that the boys seemed to be very interested in. It contained sugar cubes and stuff. Wonder what that was about . . . ?)

We weren't just three cute dancer girls with whom the Beatles hung out for a few days. Our friendships with them lasted a lifetime. (Okay, so I never talked to any of them again, except for once when I saw George at a pool in Rome. I didn't think he'd recognize me. I was writing a postcard to Toni, telling her I was watching him from across the pool, when he came over to say hello. That counts for something, doesn't it?) We returned to Los Angeles no wiser, but plenty cooler. Soon enough I got a part in another movie choreographed by David Winters. It was *Pajama*

Party, with Frankie Avalon and Annette Funicello. I was, as you might've guessed, a "pajama girl." We had just started rehearsing several musical numbers, one of which was a Watusi with Dorothy Lamour (don't ask), when the assistant director came up to a bunch of us and said, "Who can do stunt dives?" From my experience on movie sets, I knew that stunts meant more money. We pajama girls looked around at each other. No one responded. I shrugged and said, "Sure, I can do a stunt dive!"

He said, "Oh yeah? What can you do?"

I was on the spot. I'd never done a dive in my life, much less a stunt. So I said the first thing that came into my head. "I can do a . . . Blonya."

He said, "What's a Blonya?" Good question. What *was* a Blonya? I had no idea. "I can't explain it. It can only be filmed once because I go up to the end of the board and I do this . . . thing." I was clearly a brilliant, articulate, stunt-diving pajama girl.

He said, "How much do you want for it?"

Now we were negotiating.

"Five hundred dollars."

He looked at me. I weakened.

"All right, I'll do it for two hundred fifty." I had no idea what I was doing, but I could see that if I was smart and aggressive in this business, I could get further faster. So when they said, "Okay, we're rolling . . . and, ACTION!" I ran off the end of the diving board and did what felt like a double reverse somersault with six and a half twists. It ended in the most painful belly flop of my life, but that part of the dive didn't appear in the movie. When I got the $250, it felt like winning a prize.

I remember driving home from the set that night in my black and white Fairlane thinking, It's not that hard to succeed in this business. You just need to be willing to jump off the high-dive and not be afraid to belly-flop.

Another thing happened on *Pajama Party* that I'll never forget. My former teacher David Winters was choreographing the movie, and he had created a big dance number for us to do in the midst of a volleyball game. It was an intricate ballet where we threw the volleyball around while dancing. I was to be buried in the sand, and then on the fifth count of eight—five, six, seven, eight—I'd jump up, hit the ball, go down, do a rollover, and pop up again.

We rehearsed it for weeks, and I had it down perfectly. Then the day arrived when we finally went to the beach to film it. I walked to the volleyball court, where I saw the prop man digging an enormous hole in the sand. I said, "What are you doing?"

"Well, you're supposed to be buried in the sand here, so I'm digging a hole."

I looked at the hole. It was so deep that the bottom was filling with water, and the shape was a little too coffinlike for my taste. I said, "Don't you think that's too deep? I'll never get out. I need to pop up and hit the ball, you see." But he just kept digging. I started to protest, but then the assistant director came over and said, "Get in the hole. Let's try it," and then he went off to check on the other girls.

So I got down in the hole, and the prop guy buried me to my neck in the sand, which was fast turning to mud. I started to panic a little and said, as calmly as one who's being buried alive can say, "Ah, I can't move."

He looked at me blankly. Then, finally, he spoke.

"We have to put some newspapers over your head. You're not supposed to be visible."

So I was buried neck-deep in mud, newspapers covering my

head. There was no way I could get out to do my move. I couldn't even breathe. I started to freak. All of a sudden I heard the music start and I said, out loud, to myself, "We must be rehearsing." This was a complete nightmare. Through my own increasingly rapid panting I heard someone whisper from above me, "It's not a rehearsal. They're shooting." The film was running, and I was buried alive.

So what if they were shooting the stupid movie; I had reached my limit. I couldn't help it. I started yelling, "Help! Help! I can't move!" I tried to move, to escape, but it was no use.

I figured at some point someone would say, "Cut, cut, cut!" and dig me out, but no one paid any attention. They also couldn't afford to do a bunch of takes, so they just kept rolling. If you want a good laugh, rent *Pajama Party*, and watch closely. In the middle of the volleyball scene, way in the back, you'll see a poor girl emerging from the sand, spitting, waving her arms, and then sort of staggering off-camera like a drunken lobster. Then they cut to Buster Keaton in an Indian outfit, standing by a surfboard.

Whenever I think of trying to claw my way to the top, I remember that movie, and how I had to claw my way just to get to sea level.

6

Ballerina in a Go-Go Cage

By 19??, I had earned enough money to move into a better apartment. It was a beautiful, two-bedroom, one-bathroom, Spanish-style upstairs half of a duplex on Beachwood Canyon Drive in Los Angeles, and it was all mine.

My neighborhood, Beachwood Canyon, was what Nathaniel West described in *Day of the Locust* as a hodgepodge of odd characters on the fringes of Hollywood. At the time, and even now, it's where aspiring actors, writers, directors, and wannabe anythings live when they first get to Hollywood. As a kid I'd visited my parents' friends, my "uncle" Ben Wrigley (the one with the dog act) and his wife Joy, who lived at the Argyle Hotel in nearby West Hollywood with the seven or eight dogs from their act. So Beachwood was familiar territory, and I was thrilled to be part of it.

My neighbors on Beachwood were Richard Dreyfuss and Carl Borack. They shared the apartment next door. Their friends were Rob Reiner and Albert Brooks, who I remember as permanently perched on Richard and Carl's sofa. At the time, there were just four funny guys I knew—not the legendary actors and directors they would one day come to be. (Except for poor Carl, who would have to settle for a wildly successful career as, of all things, a producer.) We were all coming and going to auditions all the time. Rob, Richard, and Albert were in an improv comedy group called The Session with Larry Bishop, son of Joey. Toni, my friend Marcia, and I used to go watch them perform at a comedy club called the Improv.

Richard Dreyfuss was always busy doing theater somewhere. He used to recite *Romeo and Juliet* to me under my window. Sounds romantic, doesn't it? Whenever I stopped by his apartment, I'd find any combination of the four sitting on the couch watching TV. They used to watch old movies like *Casablanca* with the sound off and imitate the actors. Albert Brooks was by far the winner of this talent contest; he could play every character in *Casablanca* brilliantly, to the letter. I went next door frequently to enjoy the show, and they treated me like one of the guys. No flirting, no door-opening, no boy/girl BS—just good friends complaining about the horrors of show business.

Too bad I had crushes on all of them.

My idea of seduction was to throw elaborate dinner parties. I'd invite the boys next door over for dinner, then spend the whole day slaving over the stove to make my famous moussaka. But my guests were never quite as impressed as I thought they should be. They were far too busy making each other laugh to take much notice of my culinary efforts, which were goyish to say the least. (Ever hear of Miracle Whip?) It was a tough crowd, and the conversation always turned to the industry: who was casting what show, and when. The business talk was fast and furious. My guests were the young Turks, and they were more interested in their careers than, well, me, or any other girl (or so I like to think). My attempt to seduce them may have been a wasted effort, but that dinner conversation cast its own spell. It seduced me into the longest affair I'd ever have—my affair with Hollywood.

In 1965, my mother was working as a costumer on the TV series *That Girl* with Marlo Thomas. Every week she went in to the casting director, a guy named Fred Roos, and put my headshot on his desk, saying, "You should really take a look at her." Finally, Fred, who would become a friend, caved and agreed to meet me. I was embarrassed by my mother's relentless promoting, but I read for him and—voilà!—I landed an appearance on *That Girl,* guest-starring alongside my friend Rob Reiner as his girlfriend Estelle (who was named after his mother). Performing together was fun. At least the crew laughed. In my episode, Ann (that girl) got her toe stuck in a bowling ball, and Rob and I had to go out to dinner with her and her boyfriend, the wonderful Ted Bessell, pretending we didn't notice the bowling ball. So maybe Rob wouldn't date me in real life, but at least he'd date me on TV.

That Girl was a nice addition to my résumé, but, me being me, I still thought it wasn't impressive enough. I was convinced I didn't have enough theater experience, and I knew that my paltry roles in makeshift productions like *Rebel Without a Cause* at the North Hollywood Playhouse wouldn't get me the parts I wanted at credible theaters or in movies and television. So I padded my résumé with a few things I thought would make me look like a serious New York theater actress. As I said, these people needed a little nudging.

Picking Broadway plays that starred people I admired, I added them to my résumé: *Desire Under the Elms* and *The Three Sisters,* directed by Lee Strasberg and starring Geraldine Page and Terry Garr. There. That looked much better. There was no way the people casting sitcoms like *Mayberry R.F.D.*, a spin-off of *The Andy Griffith Show*, would catch on to my little fabrication. But because my mother hadn't raised a liar, I made sure to footnote my embellishment. That way, the burden of proof was on the interviewer. Next to the new credentials I put a little asterisk, and at the bottom of the résumé was a line that said simply, "*L.I.E."

Amazingly, no one ever asked me what this meant. Of course, it meant the starred credit was a lie. Hello? L.I.E. If anyone had asked about it, I was prepared to say that it meant Long Island Expressway, which was true. It didn't make sense, but neither had the Blonya, and that had given me some much-needed confidence to go in and land the parts I knew I deserved.

It also taught me that no one in Hollywood really reads. They like pictures.

And then I got my first big break as an actress. A friend in my acting class told me that they were casting a guest role on *Star Trek*, which was in its second season and already a huge hit. This role was supposed to spin off into its own series—*Assignment: Earth*. It was going to be tough to get an audition—all the big agents were clamoring to get their clients seen, and my agent wasn't in that league. She was great at making calls, but not so likely to have them returned.

Luckily, my friend from acting class had an in and helped me get through the door. I never thought I would get the part because I was still really just a dancer. Commercials and *That Girl* were small potatoes as far as *Star Trek* was concerned; they practically didn't count. I really had no credibility as an actress, except for the Long Island Expressway plays. Then I read the script and saw that in the first scene my character was flustered because she was late. I thought: Well, I'm always late. I can do late. After I did the reading they asked me to come in for a screen test. I'd never had a screen test before! They cut my hair short and put me in front of a camera. They had me turn in a circle very slowly. Then they asked me easy questions, like "What's your name?" and "Where were you born?" I was overjoyed to be having a screen test. I didn't dare hope I'd get any further, but the next thing I knew, they were calling me to appear on set. I was dizzy with joy—and that dizziness helped me get into character.

In *Assignment: Earth* Kirk and Spock travel back to Earth in the '60s in order to prevent World War III. I played Roberta Lincoln, a dippy secretary in a pink and orange costume with a very short skirt. Had the spin-off succeeded, I would have continued on as an earthling agent, working to preserve humanity. In a very short skirt. But it was not to be. The episode wouldn't air until the end of the second season of *Star Trek,* on March 29, 1968.

Star Trek was the first job where I had a fairly big (for me) speaking part. Up until then, as a dancer, I'd been treated like an extra. But suddenly everything was focused on me. As I read over my lines, one person was tugging my dress, someone else was combing my hair, and a third person was doing my makeup. I realized that I wouldn't have a moment of solitude to get into character, that dealing with those distractions was part of the job.

At the time, when an actor got a role on a TV show or in a movie, he or she would take out an ad in *Variety* to announce the appearance. It was shameless self-promotion, but it was the best way to let the industry know you were working and earning enough to afford the ad. (Now agents pay for the ads, which makes the whole thing a little more tasteful.) As the date of the show approached, I thought, This is my big break. I've got to put an ad in *Variety*. But I didn't want to use my headshot like every other actor. I wanted to do something more original.

I put it off, trying to think of just the right approach. The date got closer and closer, but still I had nothing planned. Then one day I went to the dentist (thank you, SAG, for insurance) and had my annual X-rays taken. And I thought, I know! I'll put X-rays of my teeth in *Variety*.

So I did. I bought an ad that said, "Watch Terry Garr smile on *Star Trek*" and showcased my teeth, roots and all. For the next few weeks all I heard from anyone were recommendations for dentists.

I don't know if it had anything to do with my sexy molars in *Variety*, but after I shot *Star Trek* I finally started to get real acting work. I looked for parts the same way I always had: I'd go down to the newsstand on Fridays, buy the trades, and look at the TV and movie production charts. If I found a familiar name anywhere on the charts, I'd call Coralie and ask her to send my picture to the connection. This networking had never worked miracles for me, but it had worked some, and now I was on the industry radar, so to speak, so I got cast as birdbrained lasses in *The Beverly Hillbillies, Mayberry R.F.D.,* and *Batman*. These were all small credits. In fact, they were so small that instead of calling them credits, I refer to them as debits. But I was glad for each and every one. I felt fortunate, but far from secure.

I was always hustling for the next job, and I'd started to become frustrated with the Coralie Jr. Agency, which was only helpful to a certain point. She'd let me know when parts came up, but it always took a connection beyond her to seal the deal. When I landed that coveted *Star Trek* part, I finally got real representation. My brand-new agent at the William Morris Agency gave me a single piece of advice: "Don't tell them you're a dancer—they'll think you're a whore," and then promptly ignored me. Here I was, thinking of myself as an artist and craftsman, and they were thinking "ho"?

Even though I was getting acting work here and there, dancing was still my bread and butter. For a while I danced on *Shindig!*—a rock-and-roll show where the dancers shook their thangs on little podlike stages. The musical guests were bands like Paul Revere and the Raiders, Leon Russell, and Billy Preston. I think the Rolling Stones even made an appearance once.

I was a go-go dancer, wearing a short, pleated, gray skirt (the show was in black and white, so the gray wasn't as bad as it sounds), a white T-shirt, and white knee-high go-go boots that zipped up the inside. I had several L.I.E. acting credits to my name, and still I was only prancing on a pod. We specialized in doing wacky dances like the Pony, which involved bouncing from one foot to the other and flinging one hand and then the other straight into the air; or the Watusi, which was an African butt-shaking shimmy. We'd pretend to swim and skate and mime blowing bubbles up on those pods. It was rigorously choreographed. We rehearsed eight to ten hours a day and did each move in perfect synchronicity, which was pretty ridiculous considering how humiliating being a go-go dancer was. There I was, dancing in a cage. Me, the artiste! I had been trained in classical ballet! It was not my destiny to gyrate in a cage like a monkey in the zoo!

It may not have been my destiny, but it was definitely my job for a while. After *Shindig!* I moved on to a show called *Shivaree* (which we used to call "Shit or Pee"), a precursor to MTV. It was a half-hour rock-and-roll show where real groups like the Rolling

Stones, Stevie Wonder, and Lovin' Spoonful would perform. There were four of us girls standing on pods and dancing, and a bunch of teenagers who would clap and look up at the dancers (or at least up our skirts) admiringly.

The dancing in *Shivaree* wasn't taken as seriously as it had been in *Shindig!* The cameras only panned up to show us now and then, so we did the same three steps over and over again, knowing nobody would notice or care. Between takes we'd drink gin out of paper cups and say it was water. This was starting to look like the beginning of something bad.

After I'd been there for a while, the producer invited me to be the choreographer of the show. I was flattered, but I didn't want that much of a commitment. It was kind of like when you're waitressing and they ask you to be the manager, but you really want to be a rock star. No way. Dancing was no longer my passion. It was my bread and butter. I was into punching in, dancing, and punching out.

A friend of mine who'd been in the movie version of *West Side Story,* Bobby Banas, was a great dancer and choreographer. I recommended him for the job, and soon he was my boss.

Now, during my down time on the set, I was always reading plays. One day I was lounging on my pod with a book, and Bobby said, "No reading or I'll have to fire you." And I said, "What are you, a communist?" He was my friend, I'd gotten him the job, and I knew I could get away with anything, so I ignored him. But he fired me! That was the first time I ever heard the expression "No good deed goes unpunished." Bobby's still a friend of mine, and now that I'm less young and wiser, I do see Bobby's point. I wasn't being true to my work ethic, which had always served me well—at least until the Watusi.

And that was the end of "Shit or Pee."

So much for my big break. I'd been on *Star Trek,* and now there wasn't an acting job in sight. There was, surprisingly, total silence from my new so-called agent. Then salvation came in the form of my mentor, the dance teacher David Winters, who was working on yet another Ann-Margret movie, *The Swinger.* I told him about being fired and he offered me a job as Ann-Margret's "dance-in," which is just a fancy term for body double.

It was 1966 and movies were still squeaky clean, regulated by the Motion Picture Association of America. (The ratings system wouldn't emerge until 1968, prompted by the use of the word *screw* in *Who's Afraid of Virginia Woolf?* and nudity in the Michelangelo Antonioni movie *Blowup.*) So in *The Swinger,* when they wanted Ann-Margret to act like she was drugged out, they had some beatniks hypnotize her by swinging a pocket watch in front of her face. Then they used her body as a paintbrush, rolling it in paint and then rolling it on a canvas. Except that it wasn't her body. In the long shots, it was mine. It's the most chaste orgy scene in movie history, and the paint was made of pudding mixed with food coloring. Since I'd just been fired from *Shivaree* for reading a book, I needed the job.

The director of *The Swinger,* George Sidney, had also directed *Bye Bye Birdie.* In the beginning of that movie, Ann-Margret walks in front of a landscape, singing. Sidney had her walk on a treadmill in front of a backdrop to create that scene and was delighted with the results of his special effects (this was before either treadmills or special effects were well known or high tech). So he decided to do the same thing in *The Swinger* with me.

When Ann-Margret's character woke from her trance, he

wanted to show her running in front of a blue sky, still coated in the pudding-paint. So he put me on a treadmill to shoot the scene, and I ran, and ran, and ran. They kept me running even when they were figuring out what to do next. I must have run a marathon. I was in pretty good physical shape and there was no funny tingling at that point, but it was still exhausting and kind of humiliating, running in place while the "artists" were figuring out what to do next. This gig was making *Shindig!* look like a walk in the park.

The last day of shooting, someone finally yelled, "It's a wrap." There I was, naked but for a sweaty, pudding-soaked, flesh-colored leotard, and no one even handed me a towel.

It was hard to feel like my career was going anywhere, given that I had spent so much time running in place—literally and figuratively. I had basically gone from a monkey in a cage to a hamster on a wheel. My career was tumbling down the evolutionary ladder.

As I saw it back then, I hadn't quite hit bottom. But the work was sparse, and I needed the money, so I applied for a job at Bullocks, the big department store at the time (which is now Macy's). I figured if I sold cosmetics, I could also learn about makeup, which would be good experience for a budding actress.

But there was a problem. Easy as it was for me to learn intricate dance routines in five-minute auditions, I couldn't seem to find the rhythm of the cash register. I guess my heart just wasn't in it. So yes, I got fired again. The bottom wasn't looking so far away anymore. But I always had hope.

At the time, Goldie Hawn was married to my friend Gus Trikonis. Gus had been a dancer in *West Side Story* with me, one of the Sharks. So Goldie and I hung in the same circle of performers, and everyone was always trying to help everyone else out. We'd exchange tips about recipes, clothing sales, astrologers— your basic everyday needs. Goldie told me to go to a numerologist in the Beverly Wilshire Hotel. I didn't know Goldie very well, but whatever she was doing for her career was working, and I wanted to get me some, even if it took psychics or seers or snake oil (which it often did).

So, like a sucker, I went to Goldie's numerologist, who had one critical piece of information for me upon learning that I was born Terry Ann Garr: She told me that if I wanted success, I couldn't have double letters in both of my names. She didn't offer a logical explanation. (After all, she was a numerologist.) I guess it threw my aura out of whack. Name-changing ran in my Hollywood family; both my parents had changed their names, since taking a stage name was all the rage in their generation. My mother had changed her name from Emma Schmotzer to Phyllis Lind. My father, like me, had been suckered into seeing a numerologist. But he ended up changing his name from Edward Gonnoud to Eddie Garr. Now I knew why my dad hadn't made it in spite of all his talent—too many double letters! Poor guy went to the wrong scam artist.

The numerologist told me I could be Terry Gare or Teri Garr, but not Terry Garr. "Gare" sounded too much like a French train station, so I chose the latter. Apparently, she gave this advice frequently because she had a name-change form handy. She filled it out and handed it to me, and from that moment on I was Teri Garr. It wasn't terribly sophisticated, but at least it was numerologically sound.

After I became "Teri," every time I needed to feel better about my career, I told myself, I didn't pay $35 to a Beverly Hills numerologist to change my name for nothing. I did it so my career would soar. Crazy? Most certainly. But it was the best $35 I ever spent. Soon after, as promised, things started happening for me. The very next week I visited my mother in the Valley, and we went to an army surplus store to shop for jeans. The dressing rooms were full, so I was half hiding behind the stacks of jeans, about to shimmy into a pair, when I was startled by a guy who introduced himself as Chris Bearde, a writer/producer. While I stood there in my underwear, trying to play it cool, he said, "I saw you on *Star Trek*. You're a very good actress."

Ah, yes, *Star Trek*. That excellent credit had slid from my consciousness during my mind-numbing run on the treadmill. Chris went on to tell me that he was casting a show, and was I interested in auditioning? I didn't even ask what the show was. I just said yes.

Fate visits when you least expect it, and apparently likes girls in their underwear. I went in and got the job on *The Ken Berry "Wow" Show*, and just in time. I had never worked outside of show business, except for a few years of babysitting starting when I was twelve. See, you never know.

I was saved.

7

Money Talks and Bullshit Walks

The Ken Berry "Wow" Show was a variety hour full of old-fashioned song-and-dance numbers, the kind that Ken Berry had become famous for in his *Carol Burnett Show* appearances and his Kinney shoe commercials. Ken Berry was the host, joined by me; my old Disneyland acquaintance Steve Martin; Cheryl Stoppelmoor (later Ladd), who would later become a Charlie's Angel; Laara Lacey; and Carl Gottlieb, among others. It was quite a crew. We were all just starting out, and we were glad to be working.

There were lots of bits with '40s music like "The Boogey-Woogey Bugle Boy of Company B," in which we sang and danced. Every other show seemed to feature a takeoff on a Ginger Rogers movie. I wore long dresses with feathers on the bottom and white-blond wigs. I loved getting dressed up in over-the-top costumes. It felt like I was back in the costume room at NBC, except now the costumes were made for me, and they fit perfectly. They even wrote my name in the shoes.

The show was only a six-week summer replacement for *The Mod Squad* on ABC. In those days, TV shows ran from September to May. In the summer, all shows would go off the air, and they'd either play reruns or try out new shows. Basically, we were filling in so the cast of this other show could take the summer off. But if Ken's show was a hit, ABC had promised to keep us on the air. No one really knew what to expect, except Steve, who was wrong.

I remember walking across the parking lot on my way to lunch with Steve one day, before the show was broadcast (we were still writing and taping episodes), and he said, "Look at this. We're not going to be able to do this in a couple weeks." I had no idea what he was talking about. "Once the show's on the air, we won't be able to walk across the parking lot. We'll be mobbed with fans." He was dead serious, I think.

At the end of that summer, I got a call from Chris Bearde, the lifesaving producer who'd invited me to audition for the *"Wow"* show when I was half clothed in the army surplus store. He said, "The bad news is, they're canceling the '*Wow*' show." In spite of Steve's optimism, the show was basically a flop. It ran for its allocated six weeks and then disappeared, which was too bad because there were some really talented people on that show. But the decision makers at the networks didn't care that it flopped because it was summer and everyone was sitting out on their porches watching fireworks instead of inside watching TV. The ratings weren't high enough to suit the suits, so the fun was over. But Chris Bearde went on to tell me the good news. He was also a producer on another summer replacement that *had* been picked up by CBS. He asked me to be on the *The Sonny and Cher Comedy Hour*.

Sonny and Cher had already achieved pop stardom with "I've

Got You, Babe," "The Beat Goes On," and several other hits. I thought Sonny was the real talent, but when I saw them on TV, the tables were turned. Cher was a stunning presence with her beautiful, flowing hair and her floor-length gowns. She was pure showbiz. I said, "Sure, why not?" I played it down, but I wanted that job more than anything except, well, any other job.

My job was to play sidekick to Cher's larger-than-life characters. There was a running sketch where she played a housewife, Laverne, who ran into me, Olivia, at the Laundromat. She wore big earrings and chewed gum, and I had pink curlers in my hair. I played straight man to her as she complained about her husband. Or I'd play a bride returning a shower gift to Cher in the complaint department of a store. Or we'd be part of a nutty family of trapeze artists questioned by the police in the mysterious death of Hilda the human cannonball. It was even more fun than it sounds.

I thought Cher was glamorous. She swore a lot, which I respected. But I felt no need to imitate her, and I certainly didn't feel that I competed with her in any way. It was her show, after all.

But one day on the set I caught Cher giving me the once-over. I was wearing what I always wore: jeans and a T-shirt from Orbach's on Fairfax—cheap, hip, and I thought it suited me. But it was bland compared to Cher's extravagant style. She wore long, elaborate, beaded gowns on the show, and multiple wigs through the course of the night. (She still had long hair, but the wigs were easier for quick style changes, of which there were many.) After checking me out from head to toe, Cher said, "You have to get a look. I have a look." Looking at her in her black feathers and snake boots, I thought, Yes, you sure do.

Cher's dressing room was across the hall from mine. She always had shrimp cocktails, cold Coca-Colas, and racks of extravagant costumes from which to choose. My dressing room was, as we say in show business, a nail with a hanger on it. Regardless, Cher would always come over to my room to sneak cigarettes. That was before we decided smoking was making us look old, and heaven forbid we should look old at twenty-five.

What impressed me most about Cher was that even though she and Sonny had topped the charts when "I Got You, Babe" replaced the Rolling Stones' "Satisfaction" as number one in August of 1965, she acted like one of the girls. She'd come sit down with all the dancers and talk about face cream or hairdos or men. She taught me to do needlepoint, and we'd sit around working on our pillows between scenes. When I got stuck, I always wanted to know the by-the-book way to fix my work. Cher would simply say, "You just do what you have to do. It's like life: You don't have to play by the rules. Just get it done."

When you work on a show like *Sonny and Cher*, or even "*Wow*," everyone ends up hanging out. Steve Martin and I had only crossed paths during our stints at Disneyland, but on "*Wow*," we became friends. One of the things we had in common was an interest in collecting art. Steve was more savvy about it than I was; it took me a while after my experience as Ann-Margret's stand-in not to get hives from just looking at paint. One summer day, Steve took me to some West Hollywood art galleries, and I fell in love with an Impressionist painting of a woman sitting on a bench, her head leaning on her chin. The artist was someone named Guy Pene DuBois. It was light and bright, with lots of yellow and blue, and the sign above her head said, SUFFRA-GETTE. The woman seemed disgruntled but determined, strong, and sassy. I loved it.

Steve said, "You should buy it." But it was $7,000. That was a huge amount of money to me. Still, I admired Steve, and he had once told me that I should buy art because of how it made me feel, not whether or not it matched my furniture. I connected with the DuBois painting—so, unbelievably, I shelled out my hard-earned *Sonny and Cher* money to own it.

A few years later, when I was living up on Sunset Plaza, Steve was dating Bernadette Peters, who was my downstairs neighbor. He stopped by to say hello, saw the painting, and said, "You can't have this art in here; look at this lock. You have one little lock on this door. Anyone could walk in and take that painting. It's an expensive painting."

"Quiet! Some art-loving burglar might be outside and hear you!" I said. "Yeah, okay. Maybe you're right. I'll buy another lock."

He said, "I'll buy the painting from you for seven thousand dollars."

I responded, "Well, that's what I paid for it."

He said, "Yeah, but I'm doing you a favor. I'm taking it off your hands so you don't risk losing it altogether." He had a point. Why should I make a profit when he was just trying to help me out? It sounded fair to me, so I agreed. To make a long story short, Guy Pene DuBois became very well known, and now the painting is worth about a hundred times the amount for which I bought and sold it.

I wonder what kind of locks Steve's using now. Maybe I should find out. What's a few million dollars between old friends?

After almost a year of working together, Steve asked me to do a bit for a comedy record he was making. He did the opening act for Sonny and Cher, so he had a lot of material he was recording already, but he wanted to create some additional material so he could put together a whole record. He wanted me to record a bit called "Listening to the Sounds of the Night." I met him at a recording studio, where we pretended we were sitting on a porch talking. We were having a romantic conversation, listening to the crickets and frogs, when our evening bliss was interrupted by a loud fart sound. This was one of Steve's early "sophisticated" jokes. But at the time, farting wasn't the driving comedic force that it is now; I'm sure it would be a big hit today. Steve, not surprisingly, was ahead of his time.

In addition to being a gas-inspired visionary, Steve was a wheeler-dealer. He always had some harebrained scheme he was trying to pull off. He had written a sketch for *The Smothers Brothers Comedy Hour* that he wanted to film, called "The Absent-Minded Waiter." He asked me to be in it and to find a friend to play my date, so I brought the brilliant writer and comedian Buck Henry. I had met Buck at a tennis tournament that I went to with Harry Gittes, a friend of Jack Nicholson's. (Jack Nicholson's character in *Chinatown* is named Jake J. J. Gittes.) Jack gave Harry my number, and we went out a few times. By the time I met Buck, he had already written *The Graduate* and created *Get Smart* with Mel Brooks. I was a fan, and we started a friendship that would last a lifetime.

Steve told us where and when to show up, and had everything organized to make his seven-minute film happen—studio time, a lighting director, cameras. Carl Gottlieb, our old pal from *The Ken Berry "Wow" Show,* would direct. (Steve and Carl would also go on to write *The Jerk* together.) "The Absent-Minded Waiter" was about a couple who goes to a restaurant for dinner and is served by a waiter who pours the water before the glasses are on the table, takes orders multiple times, etc. He's the most absentminded waiter in the history of time. All my character wants to know is

75

why, why, why her husband has taken her to this restaurant. Buck and I got paid in Betamaxes, those precursors to the VCR that would be obsolete about ten minutes later. But Steve Martin's little film would have a much longer shelf life. It was nominated for an Academy Award and is still something of a cult favorite.

While I was working on *The Sonny and Cher Comedy Hour,* I still auditioned all the time. When it came to my acting, I adopted the same attitude that had served me so well with *West Side Story:* I wouldn't take no for an answer. Even when it absolutely was the answer, I still didn't buy it. If I went in for a role and I heard back that I wasn't right for it, I would always say, "They made a *huge* mistake." If the word came back that I was nervous and didn't know what I was doing, I would think, Without me, that movie is going to sink like a stone. Rarely did it ever hurt my feelings. Nothing would set me back.

I came to the conclusion that if you really believe that you can get whatever you want, nothing can stop you. That was me. This attitude fueled my ambition for years. And believing made it come true. Even when life got more complicated, and what I wanted didn't fall into my lap, my faith in my own abilities kept me going.

I was the queen of excuses when it came to getting out of work to audition for the next role. I'd more than exhausted the dentist, gynecologist, and eye doctor excuses. I must have killed off at least five of my grandmothers. Then it happened that my commercial agent was working with Francis Ford Coppola to cast his new film, *The Conversation.* Coppola had already won Best Screenplay for *Patton, The Godfather* had just come out to rave reviews, and Coppola was the hottest director at the time.

When I walked into the audition, the first person I saw was

Fred Roos. A familiar face! He was a casting guy at NBC, the guy to whom my mother had given my picture and résumé, which resulted in my getting a part in *That Girl*. Fred was and always has been a great mentor to aspiring artists. He went from being a casting director to being a producer on almost all of Coppola's movies, including *The Godfather,* and here he was, greeting me warmly.

Next thing I knew, I got a call telling me that I had the part, and that the cast reading was in San Francisco the very next day. I said, "But I'm on Sonny and Cher's show. We're rehearsing a Japanese rock-and-roll opera tomorrow. I can't miss rehearsal!" They said, "You got the part. If you want it, be here tomorrow." So in I went to the assistant director of *The Sonny and Cher Comedy Hour* with yet another fake doctor's-appointment excuse. (Ironically, twenty years later I'd be using auditions as excuses to get out of doctors' appointments.)

The night before I went to San Francisco, I was so nervous about my first movie job that I single-handedly drank a six-pack of beer to calm myself down. When I flew out at 6 A.M., the beer had taken its toll. I was too sick to be nervous. I was even too sick to be sick. When I did the cast reading for *The Conversation,* I had such a headache it was all I could do to keep my head off the table. Then I flew back immediately to dance with Cher in rehearsal by 2 P.M. I was only an hour late, and I went right up onstage.

It was a long, tough day, and it changed the way I felt about drinking. At that time I didn't think of my father as an alcoholic, so I wasn't particularly concerned about my own relationship with alcohol. I'd never had the same love for booze that my father had, anyway. I just had my share of fun, like anyone else. But I had seen my father create his own obstacles, and I wasn't about to do the same.

The truth is, I was too competitive to drink much. If I drank alcohol at night, I couldn't function until about 4 P.M. the next day. I'd think, What audition did I miss today? What other blond got the job that I was too hung over to try out for? Competition, pure and simple, saved me from the drinking life.

I never drank on a work night again. It was a painless sacrifice to launch my movie career, and it was that job—my part in *The Conversation*—that figured prominently in the success that was to come.

8

What Knockers

The Conversation was about a lonely, paranoid surveillance agent named Harry Caul (Gene Hackman) who records a conversation between a man and a woman during his lunch hour in a downtown park and gets obsessed with unraveling the riddle of their exchange. I played a side character: Harry's girlfriend, Amy, who knows nothing about her lover—not his birthday; not what he does for a living. She doesn't even know when he's going to appear at her door. She spends all her time in a nondescript apartment waiting for Harry to show up. All she wants is to know him, but when she starts asking questions, he can't tolerate the invasion of his privacy and withdraws.

What can I say? It wasn't exactly a movie about female role models, but it had other merits. The movie, which came out not long after the Watergate scandal, captured the suspicion of the era, and with Coppola's clever spy-becoming-the-spied-upon twists, it was destined to become a paranoia classic.

I couldn't believe I was working with Francis Ford Coppola. *The Godfather* had just come out the year before—1972—and had been nominated for eleven Academy Awards (it won for Best Picture). *The Conversation* was nominated for the Palme d'Or, the prize for the best feature film to be awarded at the 1974 Cannes Film Festival. The Palme d'Or is one of the highest honors in filmmaking. The whole cast of the movie was invited, but nobody planned to go. Not Gene Hackman, not Harrison Ford, not Allen Garfield. I guess they were all busy, but this was my first film festival, and I wasn't about to miss it. I had no idea what to expect, but I went to Orbach's and bought myself a pretty new yellow dress made of matte jersey, a simple, scoop-necked sleeveless number that fell straight to the floor, for the occasion. It had a matching neck scarf. Very elegant.

When I arrived in Cannes, it dawned on me that I had no idea what a film festival was. (These days, even someone with a minor role would bring an entourage of assistants to Cannes.) Someone was kind enough to explain to me that you're supposed to go see all the new, hot movies. So I put on the new yellow dress, did my own hair and makeup, and went with Francis and his posse to see the movie that was the talk of the town.

I was in the south of France. I was wearing a brand-new dress. I was in Coppola's entourage, and there were paparazzi. I caught a glimpse of my reflection in the window of a café and made a funny face at myself just to stay grounded.

I settled down to watch this cutting-edge movie by Dusan Makiaiav that everyone thought was so brilliant, a Dutch film about hippies in a commune. All I remember is that the Dutch hippies got into an elevator and defecated on white plates. As we all know, art takes many forms.

Another day we went to have lunch at a villa up in the mountains where Picasso used to live. It was the middle of the afternoon and we were drinking white wine on a patio with grapevines dripping off the lattice. It was beyond belief. Several years later Francis would take his love for wine to the next level by opening a winery, but at the time we weren't thinking about business. We were too busy celebrating.

Finally, it was our big night. We entered the Palais des Festivals as a group. Once again, the yellow dress. I was just a side character, and it seemed tacky to call attention to myself. (This was before red-carpet arrivals became a bigger event than the awards themselves.) Inside, the crowd was a sea of strangers to me. I figured there were plenty of famous, powerful people, but I didn't know who any of them were. I didn't want to embarrass myself, so I kept my mouth shut, and when we took our seats I sat quietly with my hands folded in my lap.

Then came the moment when they announced the Palme d'Or. *The Conversation* had won! Francis, who was sitting right in front of me, stood up, turned around, and gestured toward me as if it were all to my credit. Was he nuts? I was onscreen for all of ten minutes. I had no idea how to respond. I just sat there with my mouth gaping open. I think I was reading too much into it because I was so nervous, but it was amazing to be in the film that won the Palme d'Or.

When I returned to L.A., I was still glowing from Cannes, and it wasn't just my Saint-Tropez tan. It was a turning point. I'd had a glimpse of movie-star life and a taste of having real roles in award-winning movies with talented actors. I was hungry for more, and I didn't want to lose any ground.

I turned my attention to the issue of my representation. I had a great manager, Pat McQueeney at Compass Management, a small but respectable management company. They'd been involved in *That Girl* when I was a guest star, and they'd asked to represent me. I said yes, of course. (I said yes to every career opportunity back then—and now, too.) Pat was a friend of Fred Roos's, and she represented Cindy Williams, Harrison Ford, Candy Clark, and a bunch of other people from *American Graffiti,* which Fred had cast. (Eventually, all of her clients left except for Harrison Ford. He stayed on as her sole client.)

So I was being managed, which was a pleasant sensation, but most Hollywood actors have a manager *and* an agent. The way it's supposed to work is that the agent gets you the auditions and the manager just yells at the agents. Something like that. The reality is that if you're hot, the money comes rolling in and everybody gets a piece. If you're not hot, they won't take your calls, but they'll still take their 20 percent. My agent at William Morris still wasn't doing anything for me. I may as well have stayed with Coralie, the process was so familiar: I'd talk my way into anything on the phone, run to any audition I could, read the trades, and listen for any tidbit that might help me land the next job.

During *The Conversation* I had met the wonderful actor Robert Duvall, who had played Boo Radley in *To Kill a Mockingbird* and Tom Hagen in *The Godfather.* I asked Robert who his agent was, and he generously fixed me up with him—Merritt Blake—when I returned from Cannes. Around the same time, my mother started doing wardrobe for a movie called *Young Frankenstein.* Mel Brooks was directing. He had just finished *Blazing Saddles* and was at the top of the comedy world. I asked my mother, as I always did, if there were any parts for me. Usually by the time they were doing wardrobe there wasn't anything left. But this time she said, "Actually, they're not done casting. You should go in."

When I called Merritt Blake to see if he could get me in to audition, he said it was a cattle call—all the agents in town were sending people, and they were seeing more than five hundred girls. He said it as if it wasn't worth my trouble. What were my chances? One in five hundred? I didn't care. When had that ever mattered? If I learned anything from my father's gambling, it was how to play the odds, and I knew that one in five hundred was better than nothing. So I have my mother, Robert Duvall, and Merritt Blake to thank for getting me into that audition.

Mel Brooks had teamed up with Gene Wilder to write *Young Frankenstein,* an affectionate parody of the Frankenstein movies of the '30s. Gene played the grandson of Dr. Victor von Frankenstein, who, after a lifetime of living down the family reputation, inherits his grandfather's castle. I was originally up for the principal female role, Elizabeth. Mel Brooks had picked me out of the hundreds of girls who came to the cattle call, but admitted that Madeline Kahn, who had been brilliant in *Blazing Saddles,* was his first choice. (I'd also seen Madeline in *What's Up, Doc?* and *Paper Moon* and thought she stole the show in both films.) Madeline didn't want the part. After *Blazing Saddles* she was tired of doing comedies and wanted her next part to be a dramatic role. But Mel was still trying to convince her. After I had auditioned three times for Elizabeth, Madeline finally accepted the role.

Of course, I was disappointed. It was a role I was dying to get, and Madeline hadn't even wanted to do it! I'd been chosen out of five hundred girls, and I'd never come so close to getting a major part in a major movie. But then Mel Brooks told me that if I came back the next day with a German accent I could read for the part of Inga—Gene Wilder's buxom love interest. I said, "Yah, I zertainly can."

A German accent in twenty-four hours. Okay! I sure wished I'd stayed in college long enough to master the accent. Luckily, I was still on *The Sonny and Cher Comedy Hour,* and as fate would have it, Cher's wig stylist was a German woman named Renata, complete with a thick guttural accent. The next day I made small talk with her all through Cher's hairstyling session. (Needless to say, that gave me hours of study.) I emerged with confidence, determination, and a perfect German accent when saying, "Mein Gott, zis vig veighs forty poundz."

There was one last thing I needed for Inga. Or two, to be exact. When I read the part, I realized it was really all about boobs, and I was not about to let my lack of them hinder my performance. The next day I went in to do my imitation of Renata for Mel Brooks wearing a fuzzy pink sweater and a huge padded bra stuffed with socks. People pay more than $5,000 for a boob job today. Mine cost under $5 at Woolworth's, and it was money well spent.

I read Inga's lines with Mel while the other producers watched. Everyone laughed! But when I finished, they said nothing more than "Thank you very much." So I did what I often did at the end of auditions—I asked if they wanted the script back. (Someone once told me if they said, "Keep the script," it was a good sign.)

So I said to Mel, "Would you like your script?"

"Nah, keep it," he said. It wasn't an offer, but it was something. I walked proudly down the hall, hoping for the best, my homemade fake boobs leading the way.

The day after the audition I was back at work, rehearsing with

Cher. I kept checking in for messages or calls, but strangely, the phones were utterly silent all day. I thought, Wow, I must have done worse than I thought. Not only am I not getting the part, they've cut off all phone calls to the entire region. It turned out that, as luck would have it, the phones at CBS were down, a technological glitch that seems impossible today but was par for the course at the time. So at 6 P.M. when I got home I called my (human) answering service, who told me that my manager, Pat Mc-Queeney, had called several times and that she had "exciting news."

I knew what that meant! I called Pat back and she affirmed the good news. I got the part! I was beside myself with joy. This was it. I'd been chosen by one of the best.

I got to thinking that I should have stuffed my bra with socks for every audition.

That night, I called Toni and all my other friends to tell them the news. I was practically convulsing with excitement. At work the next day I went across the hall to Cher's dressing room and burst out, "I got a part in a Mel Brooks movie!" She looked at me blankly and asked, "What's that?" Cher lived in a different world.

I was happy that my mother and I were working on the same movie, and I guess she was, too. But after a week of shooting I wanted to tell Mel that she was my mother—I thought he'd appreciate the connection. But my mother said, "Oh, no, no, you don't need to do that." I suppose she thought there was some sort of divide between cast and crew. I ignored her and told Mel, anyway. He looked at my mother and said, "You must be so proud," to which she answered shyly, "Yes, I am." For someone who was determined to see me in the spotlight, she sure didn't want it for herself.

Before I knew it I was in with the funny people. I was working with Mel; Madeline Kahn; Kenny Mars, who'd appeared with Madeline in *What's Up, Doc?* and *Paper Moon;* Marty Feldman, a TV writer and stage actor who'd appeared in the summer replacement TV series *The Marty Feldman Comedy Machine;* Peter Boyle, who'd played a bigot in the movie *Joe* and is best known today for his role as Frank Barone on *Everybody Loves Raymond;* Cloris Leachman, who'd won Best Supporting Actress for her role in *The Last Picture Show;* and Gene Wilder, who'd already been nominated for an Oscar for his performance as Leo Bloom in Mel Brooks's *The Producers.* Every night when I went home my laugh muscles were tired. There is a scene in which Madeline Kahn arrives at the castle and Gene Wilder says, "Can you help me with these bags?" and Marty Feldman says, "Yeah, you take the blonde and I'll take the one with the turban." Gene Wilder just laughs right through the scene. Look for it the next time you watch *Young Frankenstein.* It was impossible to get him to do it with a straight face.

Working with Mel was all fun and games. There was no formality to the proceedings. He was open to ideas from anyone— cast and crew—at any time. He'd say, "Come on, help me out. What does she say here?" and everyone would throw out suggestions. Then he'd wave his hand and say, "Okay, don't help me anymore." I used to tell him, "You're funny because you're Jewish. I wish I were Jewish." The fact is, at that point in my life my boyfriends were always Jewish (I don't know why), and Mel knew this and called me their "shiksa dream." So Mel would say, "Don't worry about it, honey. You're Jewish by injection." I can say that now that my mother isn't around to hear it.

There is a scene in the movie where Gene Wilder (as Dr. Frederick Frankenstein) and I approach enormous castle doors. Dr. Frankenstein says, "What knockers," and I say, "Oh, zank you, doctor." Now, as I mentioned, I was already enhancing my natural assets with various household objects in order to do Inga's bosom justice. But when that scene came up, Mel told my mother that we needed a bra with runways—something designed by Howard Hughes, maybe? We stuffed everything in my dress—socks, tissue, canned hams, whatever was handy. When the movie came out, people would come up to me on the street just to say, "What knockers," and they still do so today. Every so often a woman will drag her husband up to me and say, "My husband wants to say something to you. Go on, honey." Embarrassed, but on cue, her husband will mutter, "What knockers," and they will both titter like schoolgirls.

Young Frankenstein became a comedy classic. In the *New York Times* in 1974 Vincent Canby called it "Mel Brooks's funniest, most cohesive comedy to date." And, yes, it was the one that put me on the map. For one thing, it was the first major role in which I actually got to talk—not just dance, as I'd done in the Elvis movies, or get buried in sand, as in *Pajama Party*. And Mel Brooks had chosen me over so many other actresses, including every good-looking starlet who ever got off the bus in Hollywood. (Even Farrah Fawcett tried out, but within months she became one of Charlie's Angels, so I guess everything worked out for her, too.)

For the first time in my life, I went home at night and thought, I've done it. If this is as far as I get, I'll be happy. I thought I'd made it up the tough climb that every young actress knows awaits her. It takes a little luck, a lot of phone calls, and hard, hard work, no matter what anyone tells you.

I had no idea that the toughest challenges ahead of me would have nothing to do with my career.

I try to imagine what the Teri who had just completed *Young Frankenstein* and was full of youthful optimism would have said if someone had told her, "Here is the worst of what awaits you: Thirty years from now, you'll go to sleep in a hotel room, prepared to give a speech the next day. You'll wake up at five A.M. to go to the bathroom. But when you sit up in bed, you'll be hot, sweaty, and feverish.

"You'll think it's just the side effects from a shot you've taken. That's right, you'll be taking medicine three times a week to combat multiple sclerosis. You'll tell yourself it's no big deal, that some Tylenol will fix it and it'll be gone when you wake up in the morning.

"But when you stand up, you'll immediately feel weak and collapse to the floor. This will be a new feeling. You'll lie on the floor, thinking, Well, this is different. You'll try to think happy thoughts as you wriggle your way to the bathroom. When you finally approach the bathroom, you'll haul yourself into a sitting position, only to fall back and hit your head on the wall like a rag doll. Sexy. You'll notice that there's no phone within reach. You don't know who to call, anyway—the concierge? The front desk? The doors are locked with the hotel chains. While you contemplate your fate, you will drag yourself into the bathroom because that was your original reason for waking up, remember?"

The truth is that the person I was then would have no response to that vision of the life I live now. Or, more likely, she'd have said,

"Thanks for the information, but you are *so* wrong." When youth and success come hand in hand, it's not like you sit there saying, "Gee, what if this doesn't last forever?" I might have taken the time to evaluate Gene Wilder's haircut or Marty Feldman's googly eyes, but I wasn't exactly contemplating the meaning of life.

9

We're Circus People

After *Young Frankenstein,* I went back to New York to try to justify the L.I.E. credits I'd faked on my résumé. I guess I felt guilty for pulling the wool over everyone's eyes. Well, not really; in truth, I did it to be a real actress. Back in the day, to prove you were a real actress, you had to act in New York, the heart of the theater world—not just pretend that you did. Marlon Brando, Meryl Streep, Bette Davis, Anne Bancroft—they all did and/or continue to do theater. (It's not the same today. Johnny Depp and Hilary Duff don't have to act on Broadway to prove their mettle. It's still well respected, but it ain't what it used to be.) Ten years after the last mistake I ever made (recall the admittedly flubbed *grande jeté* in 1964), I was back, but this time I was determined to make more of the experience.

In Hollywood, I had studied a bit with the internationally renowned teacher Lee Strasberg. When I got to New York early in 1974, I immediately went to the Actors Studio, where he was the artistic director, to see if I could continue. Turns out it wasn't quite that easy. The Actors Studio was so hot that in order to get one of the coveted slots in the courses, I would have to audition, and the auditions took place only once a year. There wouldn't be another Studio audition until September, which was eight months away.

So the director agreed to let me "observe" during that time. I'd audit the morning sessions from eleven to one, then go to Joe Allen's on Forty-sixth Street and Eighth Avenue to drink bad coffee, smoke cigarettes, and contemplate the meaning of life with my fellow actors. This camaraderie was also a big part of being an actor. Al Pacino was the star student at the Actors Studio; my old acquaintances Gene Hackman and Dustin Hoffman also dropped in occasionally. Al had been cast as a race-car driver in a movie called *Bobby Deerfield,* but there was one problem: He didn't know how to drive. He didn't even have a driver's license. So he rented a car and I gave him driving lessons. But he was hopeless. Or maybe I was a hopeless teacher. We'd be driving around Manhattan late on a Sunday night, and I'd be more concerned about the safety of the neighborhood we were in than whether he knew how to use the turn signal. Not that any of the cabdrivers noticed as he swerved from lane to lane. He may not have learned enough from me to play a race-car driver, but I taught him the main principles of Manhattan driving: Lock the doors, go as fast as you can, and no, you do not want your windows washed. He, in turn, taught me a great respect for acting.

My two favorite people from the Actors Studio were Alfa-Betty Olsen and Marshall Efron, a writing team who were restaurant critics for Manhattan's *SoHo Weekly News* and had written several children's books together. They had also written and appeared in the Emmy-winning *The Great American Dream Machine,* which was an innovative magazine show on PBS, and Alfa-Betty had worked with Mel Brooks on *The Producers*. She knew I'd just finished working with Mel on *Young Frankenstein,* so she introduced herself. Their writing project at the time was a musical comedy set in a hospital called *Hospital City*. The playwrights' unit always came over to the actors' unit looking for people to cast, and Betty and Marshall wanted me for *Hospital City*. The musical never quite took off—it was tough to do the Charleston while hooked up to an IV. Oh well I'm always ready to do their next musical, *Mental Hospital City*.

I settled quickly into my New York life, going to auditions, running in Central Park. Along with doing lots of plays, I saw lots of shows, off-Broadway and at the Public Theater. Most of the actors I knew were bicoastal, jetting between New York and Los Angeles for business meetings, auditions, and sometimes parties. I'd meet up with Marshall and Alfa-Betty or my friend Tom Schiller, who happens to be one of the funniest men on earth, at the Cedar Tavern off Union Square. Tom was one of the original writers on *Saturday Night Live,* and at the time he was doing short movies called "Schiller's Reel" on *SNL*. Probably the most memorable was the one called "Don't Look Back in Anger," in which John Belushi dances on the graves of *SNL* cast members Gilda Radner, Laraine Newman, Jane Curtin, Garrett Morris, Bill Murray, Chevy Chase, and Dan Aykroyd. Tom stayed at *SNL,* off and on, until 1993, and in the late '80s would have his own segment called "Schillervision."

In his wacky way, Tom was always cooking up adventures for us, which he called "Tom Schiller's New York." We'd take a train to Sleepy Hollow and look for Ichabod Crane, or we'd go to Staten Island in the middle of the night for no reason whatsoever. At the end of August he and I decided to have a beatnik theme party at his apartment off Washington Square Park. We told our friends to show up at his place wearing all black, and we read from Ezra Pound's *Noh,* a translation of medieval Japanese poetry, while people played bongo drums. We were five years too late for Woodstock, but I'm always late.

But on an empty afternoon when there was no audition to occupy my mind, I'd take the subway up to Bloomingdale's on Lexington Avenue and take the elevator directly to the fourth floor, where I'd walk through the beautiful displays of great cozy couches, elegant chairs, and bedroom sets with big, fluffy beds. There were even kitchens with plastic fruit on the counters. They reminded me of the television stages where my mom had worked, which made me feel safe because everything in this make-believe world was perfect and unchanging. I'd sink into a leather armchair, close my eyes, and pretend it was my house. If a salesperson approached me, I would say, "I'm just looking," or ask, "How much is that couch?" to disguise my true purpose. The rest of the world would disappear, and I'd relax in my lovely home, slip away into my imaginary life of luxury. I did this more times than I'm willing to admit.

I didn't need a shrink to point out that my perfect-house fantasy traced back to my gypsy youth, to the time when I was ten years old and we were living in North Hollywood, a place I loved, and in a house I loved (the one where my friends and I had played with our dolls on the porch). We were forced to move because we had no money, despite the fact that it seemed my parents had tried everything, including renting out our front rooms. I got attached to that house, and to the kids I skated with in the neighborhood, and to the neighbors who came to watch our garage-theater performances, more so than any other house we lived in. It was a real home to me. I had never made a fuss about our lifestyle. I didn't mind the garage-sale lamps or the dollhouses made out of rocks. But selling our house was too much. Summoning every ounce of drama in my ten-year-old soul, I'd cried and screamed and tried to talk sense into my mother. But there had been no choice.

Soon we moved to a much smaller house a short distance away. On moving day, I went through our empty old house and kissed every wall good-bye.

That disappointment and the lack of options, that feeling of being held hostage by our financial state—these were feelings that would motivate me in the coming years to never be so helpless again.

When I think back on those years, I try to imagine how my mother must have felt, watching her only daughter's heart break. But it wasn't her style to respond to such fits of emotion. She was convinced that our lives were utterly complete. She was a tough woman with strong ideals. If I came home and wanted a new doll or special shoes to match my dress, my mom would say, "Terry, you don't need that. We're circus people. We don't need what other people need." Circus people didn't care about material things. They valued experience over acquisition. They didn't live by other people's rules. My mother taught us to be proud no matter what we had or what we looked like, as long as we were good people with real friends and interesting experiences. Fortunately, we had a lot of both. I didn't have the heart to tell my mother that we weren't in the circus.

Years later, while I lounged in the comfort of my Bloomingdale's living room, I still had faith in my mother's ideals. It wasn't the fancy furniture I longed for; it was the security of home that the furniture represented. This ritual kept me grounded and believing that I was moving forward. And always, after indulging my furniture fantasy, I would go downstairs to the lunch counter and get a frozen yogurt with strawberries on top.

In New York I did anything in the theater that I could. My strangest role was in a play by Len Jenkin, called *Gogol*, which we performed at the reputable Public Theater on Lafayette Street. It was about Dr. Franz Mesmer, a native of Vienna who pioneered hypnotic therapy, and Gogol, the nineteenth-century Russian novelist who, for the purposes of the play, was his patient. It was an ensemble piece: Mandy Patinkin played an inventor, and Carol Kane was in it, too, as—if I remember correctly—a fairy. I think I played a nurse, not that it was relevant to the stunts the director asked us to perform, which included flying across the stage harnessed to a pulley. As we glided through the room, we would exclaim crazy things like "Whoooooo are youu-uuuuuu?" Then we would fly out, as though our mere presence somehow explained the inane lines we'd just delivered. At one point, actors dressed as penguins would appear, waddling and flapping their wings at their sides. It was completely bizarre.

And it was just the kind of serious credit my résumé lacked.

In the middle of rehearsals for *Gogol* (yes, we actually rehearsed) my agent—by this time it was Guy McElwayne—called from Los Angeles asking if I wanted to come back and do a movie. I replied in my grandest voice, "I'm in a play at the Public Theatah with some of the world's most renowned penguins. I can't . . ." But then he said, "They'll give you forty thousand dollars and a trailer in Burbank."

To which I replied, "Just a minute, let me put Ms. Garr on the phone."

The part was in a movie called *Oh, God!* also starring John Denver as a grocery clerk who encounters a cabdriver (George Burns) who claims to be God, the gist being that God is in everybody. I liked the idea. The role I was up for was John's exasperated, disbelieving wife. If I was open to it, John Denver wanted to meet me. I have to confess that I was a little snooty about working with John Denver. I fancied myself a hoity-toity actress, doing a cutting-edge play at the Public Theater. Did I really want to throw it all away to do a movie with a pop-music idol? Had I not evolved at all from my Elvis-movie days?

John, whom I knew had had some success with the hits "Take Me Home, Country Roads" and "Rocky Mountain High," happened to be doing a concert in New York at Madison Square Garden, and I was told to meet him there. I clearly had no idea what to expect, considering I hadn't really followed his career that closely. When I arrived, thousands of people and throngs of groupies were screaming and crying; press people were jockeying for interviews. It was wild, and I was totally blown away by his popularity.

I remember thinking, Wait a second, this guy must be some big shot. Then he started to sing. In the middle of New York City, in the huge hall of Madison Square Garden, I found his simple, clear voice and homespun songs so heartfelt that I melted. Afterward, I went to his dressing room to meet him and found him to be a gentle, pure spirit. So what if he wasn't an actor? He connected with his audience in a profound way, and he seemed to know how to make people happy.

So I considered my options: I could stay in New York, freeze my butt off in a blizzard every few days, and do a play where I flew through farts at the Public Theater. Or I could go to Los Angeles, where it was sunny and warm, do a cute movie starring John Denver, get paid $40,000, and eat shrimp cocktail in my trailer.

That was a toughie. I was on the next plane to L.A.

On top of working with someone as sweet and talented as John, it turned out that my old friend Rob Reiner's father Carl was to direct *Oh, God!* He'd known me for a long time through Rob, and he treated me like a daughter. He was skilled and gracious with John Denver, who had never done a movie before. And then there was the legendary George Burns. Never a fan of small talk, he once told me, "You have to exercise. I walk around my yard five times every morning. How do you think I keep in such good shape?" He was always saying, "Come on, let's move it. I've got a card game waiting." His card-playing buddies were always expecting him at the Hillcrest Country Club in Beverly Hills. The minute he finished his scenes he was gone. But he did invite me to his eighty-first birthday party that year. It was a big Hollywood party at producer Jerry Weintraub's house in Beverly Hills. As a present, I brought George a crystal star. He sent me a note saying, "The next time we do a picture together I'm going to insist that we do at least three or four love scenes—maybe six." I'm sure he said that to all the girls.

After my embarrassingly snobby reservations about doing the movie, it turned out that I loved hanging out and working with John Denver. Once he took me up in a plane he was piloting. I was nervous, but he was very self-assured and calming. He told me about his father, "Dutch" Deutschendorf, who had been an airforce pilot in World War II and taught John how to fly. We flew from L.A. to Aspen, where John wanted us to attend a charity ski tournament. I told him I couldn't ski, but he said it didn't matter. When we got to the mountain, we took the ski lift to the top, put some skis on, and took pictures. After we'd made our appearance, it was time to go back down the hill. But the ski lifts weren't running anymore. So I asked John, a bit nervously, "How am I supposed to get down?"

He said, "Just ski down!" I reminded him that I had no idea how to ski. "Just go for it!" he said, and took off down the hill without me. "Go for it"—that was his mantra.

What could I do? I went for it. It took me about an hour to inch down what John disparagingly referred to as a "bunny" slope, after which I gained new respect for bunnies. But by the time I got to the bottom I had the hang of it. If a bunny could do it, so could I.

Oh, God! was widely distributed and well received. I'd been in several popular movies by then, but my family paid very little attention to my fledgling career. The days when I lived with my mother and came home to her inquisitions about my casting calls were long over. She'd settled into a blasé attitude about my success. I'd get a part, each bigger than the one before, and she'd say, "That's nice, dear." Why make a fuss? As far as she was concerned, I was just doing the work I was born to do. I'm sure I was living her dream, or, at the very least, my father's, but she would never cop to it. As for my brothers, they had taken my father's advice. He always told them, "Don't be in this business. It's humiliating." So they discarded showbiz for what they saw as a better life. They were both married, living in the suburbs. But I visited them there, and those visits soon came in handy.

On the heels of *Oh, God!* Steven Spielberg cast me in *Close Encounters of the Third Kind.* He had just done *Jaws* and I was eager to work with him. I assumed that Steven had seen me in *Oh, God!* but it turned out he'd noticed me in a coffee commercial and thought I'd make a good Indiana housewife. In the movie I'm a pragmatic mother who grows increasingly frustrated with and alienated from her husband (my old neighbor, Richard Dreyfuss) as he becomes obsessed with a UFO.

I had no idea what it was like to be a beleaguered housewife. My mother never cleaned or waited for her husband to get home. She was too busy chasing him down or working to pay off his debts. But in New York, I'd taken a class with Stella Adler called Script Breakdown, in which we went through *Death of a Salesman* line by line, figuring out everything we could about the characters. I set out to model myself on the only housewife I knew—my older brother's wife, Bunny.

Thankfully, Bunny wasn't beleaguered by an alien-obsessed husband, but she *was* raising two small kids in a house in the Valley. I visited her with a journal in hand and wrote down conversations she had with the neighbors. I heard her say things like "Put that down; it's not a toy," and "Is that where your socks live, on the floor?" and Steven let me use them in the movie. I loved that he made it a collaborative effort. I even went to the closest Sears and pretended I was shopping for a refrigerator. I told the wardrobe person I wanted only polyester clothing. I was determined to get every detail right.

Filming with my old friends Richard Dreyfuss and Bob Balaban was so perfect. We'd always loved working together. But mostly, when I think of *Close Encounters,* the person who most comes to mind is François Truffaut. The legendary French filmmaker made a rare acting appearance in the film as a kindly French scientist. While we were filming, the cast and crew stayed at a Holiday Inn in Mobile, Alabama. One day I was sitting alone, eating the usual "set food" of chicken breasts in some generic milky sauce with rice, when François walked over to me and said, "May I seet wiz you?"

I said, "Yes, of course."

"You were ze girl in *Young Frankenstein Jr.?*"

"Yes, I am."

"Would you like to ave dinere tonight?"

"Yes, yes, yes!" I swooned. He was so handsome and charming and smart. And let's face it, I was naive and starstruck. That night at dinner he told me that he had written a book about his friend, the irascible Alfred Hitchcock. He said, "I call him Hitch," and I responded, "Yeah, well, I call him Cock." François laughed, and I was quite pleased with myself for having amused the great François Truffaut. (Wasn't I provocative?)

He said that whenever he made a movie, it was like a death. Something ended in his life, something changed irrevocably. And that it didn't make him sad, it made him awestruck by the power of art. Interesting, *n'est pas?* After all these years, I recall things he said to me almost every day.

I was totally taken with him. There I was, immersed in my study of acting, and François was creative, opinionated, and accomplished. He was definitely one of my teachers. He'd found critical and commercial success with *The 400 Blows* and had gone on to make many great films, including *Shoot the Piano Player* and *Jules and Jim.*

The thing about Truffaut that really fascinated me was his background. He told me stories about his convoluted childhood— his mother never married; he never knew his father. Tough stuff. (*The 400 Blows,* his first film, was just a chronicle of his early life as a bad boy.) His childhood was worse than mine. And I remember thinking, If he can do it, I can do it. Do what? Well, express myself somehow. I'd mostly, secretly, thought of myself as unfit for public consumption, having come from show business, from vaudeville, and having grown up like a weed. It inspired me to see that someone could get past that stuff and function so incredibly. (George Harrison once said the same thing to us: "Just go ahead and make things. Use yourself, anyone can do it." Of course, he was a Beatle.) I'm really not comparing myself to him, or to anyone else. I'm just acknowledging my awe, so I don't sound like a total groupie . . . just about three-eighths groupie, maybe.

François and I were on the movie set pretty much every day, so our relationship was limited to dinners and evenings. In boring old Mobile, Alabama, I looked forward to spending time with him, hung on to every story he told me and compared them to my life. Then I had a break in filming *Close Encounters*. I went back home to Los Angeles to rest, and François stayed in Mobile. Two weeks later, I returned to the set to film the rest of my scenes and to see François again. I don't know what I was thinking, leaving him alone for two weeks. Maybe my brain had been abducted by one of those aliens in the movie. But by the time I returned, he had moved on to a stunt girl.

More than being in love with him, I wanted to *be* him. I wanted to use the experiences from my life as fuel for my art, in the same way he used his.

I finished the film and left, but for years I saved the books he gave me and the notes he wrote me. One yellowed note that came under the door of my hotel room during that time ends, "Anyway, if I don't see you this morning or at lunch, I will call you as soon I will come back in order to kiss you as usual, my tenderness, lovely, fondly, François." I was so in love with him (and his broken English; I once tried to teach him to say "Bullshit," but he could only remember "bowl of shit"—not the same). I taught him some English and he taught me some French, and a whole lot more.

The clichés of showbiz relationships really did take me by surprise that time, and over and over again. I just never got used to the idea. Years later I was at the Plaza Athenee in Paris filming *To Catch a King* with Robert Wagner and I got a message to call François. I didn't call him back. Oh, I thought, *now* he wants to see me, when it's convenient for him. I thought, Forget it, he doesn't deserve to see me again. I had no idea how ill he was.

Two weeks later I heard that he'd died. I wished I had called him. I learned a big lesson with that: People come and go in life, but when the ones who really matter resurface, it's best to let bygones be bygones and focus on the good.

Except in the case of a few absolute bastards, but more on them later.

Fred Roos, my mentor who'd produced *The Conversation,* called me soon after I finished *Close Encounters.* He was producing another movie for Coppola: *The Black Stallion,* with Mickey Rooney. Fred helped me get the part of the mother of the lead boy.

When we were shooting the movie, we were stuck in a remote location outside Toronto, Canada. It was a cold, rainy spring, and I had no dressing room. It was a nightmare. I was upset because I had to change my clothes in the back of a truck. Diva? Maybe, but come on, the back of a truck? I had no place to chill out, so I complained to Fred Roos. Mickey Rooney overheard me, and he said to Fred, "Don't worry, I'll straighten her out. I straightened out Ava [Gardner], I can handle her."

Next thing I knew, Mickey called me into his dressing room and started telling me, "This is showbiz. We roll with the punches. It could be worse. Why, I remember the time we were doing a split week in Philly . . ." Blah, blah, blah. I was used to his kind of vaudeville philosophizing. And the whole time he was giving me his little pep talk, he had his radio on in the background. He was listening to the horse races. Every once in a while, he'd stop right in the middle of a sentence and say, "Hold on . . . I think I just placed . . . Damn, no, forget it . . . Okay, so when I was doing *Boys Town* I really thought I should have been the priest . . . Jeeeeeeeez, my horse just lost. Damn!" Once Mickey started talking he never stopped, even as he checked the ponies. Of course, I still had to change in the truck.

Working with Coppola was more intense for me this time since I didn't have my day job with Sonny and Cher to distract me. Carroll Ballard, the director, gave us lots of freedom to develop our parts. I wrote volumes—scenes and dialogue—about my character, Alec's mother. I wanted her to be a strong woman of the '40s, a widow but real tough, a brilliant piano teacher. At one point Carroll called me over and gently reminded me, "Teri, this is a story about a boy and a horse. It's not about his mother." I loved that woman I created, and most of her wound up on the cutting-room floor. But it was in making *The Black Stallion* with Coppola that I discovered that all that background work was a critical part of the creative process. No matter how little of the complexity survived, if she came alive for me, it was far more likely that she'd come alive for the audience, even in some small way.

I was on a roll, and it felt good. I went from *The Black Stallion* to my third Francis Ford Coppola movie, *The Escape Artist,* which starred Griffin O'Neal as a young, Houdiniesque escape artist. It was the summer of 1981, and we shot the movie in Cleveland, where my aunt (the one we'd once lived with) still lived. When I went to visit her, I couldn't help but think about living in my grandfather's attic, and the Anne Frank girl I'd imagined myself to be.

When I walked up into that attic, now filled with boxes and old furniture, I was that five-year-old girl again. But now I could reassure my five-year-old self that everything would be okay.

IO

One from the Heart

Just before I did *Tootsie,* I got the lead female role in Francis Ford
Coppola's *One from the Heart.* Nearly ten years earlier, Coppola
had given me a small role in *The Conversation,* my first big movie.
In *The Black Stallion* and *The Escape Artist,* he'd offered me mid-
sized roles. And now, at last, the award-winning director saw me
as a lead. Finally, someone agreed with me besides my mother!

Francis was coming off *Apocalypse Now* (which won the Palme
d'Or and scored eight Oscar nominations, winning for Best Cine-
matography and Best Sound) and, before that, *The Godfather*
(which swept the Oscars with Best Picture, Best Screenplay, Best
Actor, and eight other nominations). Both movies were huge critical and popular successes. After those massive hits, Francis sought
more control over his work and had the notion that he would re-
create the studio system of the '30s and '40s, free from the mass-
market mentality of the big studios in the '70s and, now, the '80s.
He envisioned an alternative studio where a stable of directors,

105

writers, cinematographers, and actors would, under one roof, work together as a repertory company. So he bought an old studio in the heart of Hollywood and commenced his debut project.

This movie, *One from the Heart*, was to be Zoetrope Studios' debut. There was tremendous pressure on him, and, by extension, on all of the cast and crew, to prove his concept and realize his dream. Could he turn out another big hit as an independent producer?

I loved *One from the Heart* from the moment I first read the sweet and lyrical script by Armyan Bernstein. It was about a couple of blue-collar lovers living together in a little house in Las Vegas, trying to figure out their lives. My character, Frannie, was an agent at a travel agency who felt like she wasn't living her life to the fullest. Her complacent boyfriend, Hank, was played by Frederic Forrest, with whom I'd worked on *The Conversation*. (He was a favorite of Francis's. He also appeared in *Apocalypse Now* and *Hammett* for Zoetrope.)

In the movie, Frannie and Hank have a fight about the anniversary presents they give each other. She buys them plane tickets for a vacation he doesn't want to take; he's spent their money on the title to their rented bungalow, which she dreams of escaping. They split up and venture out into the wilds of Vegas, where they soon encounter their fantasy mates. Frannie's is a waiter who dreams of being a pianist, played by the remarkable Raul Julia, with whom I'd also worked in *The Escape Artist*. He flirts with me through the window of the travel agency until I agree to meet him at his piano bar. Meanwhile, Hank watches a dance performed in a gigantic martini glass and falls for the femme fatale dancer, played by the beautiful Nastassja Kinski, who had to learn to walk a tightrope for another scene in the movie.

Coppola set out to tell a simple love story in an unusual manner. *One from the Heart* was a sort of jazz operetta, where the soundtrack did a lot of the storytelling. The raspy-voiced musician Tom Waits, whose debut album *Closing Time* had just come out, wrote and sang the score, accompanied by Crystal Gayle. My favorite line from one of the songs he wrote went, "I've told you before, and I'll tell you again, you can't defrost the icebox with a ballpoint pen." That line always reminded me of my crappy apartment on Gower Street where I first lived. The refrigerator had one of those tiny freezers that filled with frost at least once a month. I always chipped away at it with a knife and worried that I'd break one of the tubes until I decided, The hell with it—let it freeze over.

We started rehearsing in the spring of 1980. Francis had scheduled a three-month rehearsal period, which was unusual for a movie at that time. Usually a week before you start shooting you get together with the other actors to read through the script, but each actor is expected to come to the read-through having already researched his or her character. It's nothing like a play—which, given my *Gogol* experience, I knew oh so much about—where you develop the characters simultaneously, together. In contrast, movie producers hope that by putting actors on location, the realistic circumstances and the actors' fresh relationship to the script will make their responses more believable. Francis went beyond this. We even traveled to Las Vegas and videotaped all of our scenes in cars, Laundromats, and people's houses. Very exotic.

But Francis wanted a more theatrical approach to the material. I suppose he thought that rehearsing, improvising, and exploring our characters together would give the movie a feeling of depth—a complexity behind the love story. The actors had varied responses to this experimental approach. Some were hesitant to rehearse full-out because they were saving it for the camera. After all, how can you act in the moment if you've done the same performance a hundred times already, in front of the same less-than-inspiring camera lens? Back in the '60s, right after *Viva Las Vegas,* I'd danced in what would now be seen as a politically incorrect comedy called *John Goldfarb, Please Come Home,* starring Shirley MacLaine. Shirley would say, "I ain't doing it full-out until that old box starts grinding." I *think* she was talking about the camera.

The part of the movie I was most excited to shoot was the dancing. There were several numbers to be done: one a tango, and another a dream ballet. The amazing Gene Kelly, one of my childhood heroes, was brought in to choreograph these numbers. We were going to dance down the Las Vegas strip in the middle of a Fourth of July celebration. I hadn't danced in a movie in ten years! While we rehearsed, they started building the sets. I came to work one hot July day and saw the crew pouring cement slabs. They were re-creating an entire Las Vegas block for the huge "dancing in the street" scene. I knew this was where I'd do my dance with Raul.

The street appeared on the lot literally overnight, and it was amazingly realistic, lined with fake storefronts and dazzling neon signs. It was Vegas, baby! I knew Francis would be thrilled. But all I could think of was the Equity rule: no tap-dancing on cement. All dance floors are made of wood because it has some give to it. Cement is so solid and unyielding that it kills a dancer's legs. You could get busted by the union for making people dance on cement. But Francis made his own rules, and if he was determined to re-create a Vegas street, down to the last concrete block, he'd do it. And I wasn't about to make a fuss. Rule or no rule, I was a professional, and I would tolerate anything for my career and, especially, for Francis.

When the time came to dance down that street, I did it. Again and again, day after day. I wore a low-cut red dress, Raul wore a bow tie, and we tangoed down the bright strip surrounded by sailors, showgirls in star-spangled bikinis, revelers, and fireworks. I was doing the best work I could, for one of the most celebrated directors in history. This was a good job. Francis gave us great freedom and time to really work with our characters. And Zoetrope Studios was such an idealistic place to be. We all worked together, as a community, and it felt like history was being made. Francis was pioneering new technology throughout the filming. While most directors stood next to the camera to direct the actors, Francis holed up in an Airstream trailer to watch the scenes on video—which was a technological breakthrough he called "previsualization"—and talked to us over a loudspeaker. He is a remarkable director, always experimenting and taking risks. The press and the industry were obsessed with Zoetrope. People like Steven Spielberg, Jerry Garcia, and Norman Lear were always visiting the set. One day I looked around and there were George Lucas, Michael Powell, Jean-Luc Godard, Wim Wenders, Gene Kelly, Francis, and Akira Kurosawa. I thought, Nice group! Francis hosted a party there every Friday night. It was *the* place to be.

One from the Heart, which was *supposed* to be a big hit, was released while we were shooting *Tootsie*. There I was, on the set, thinking my big movie was about to come out and dreaming of riding in limos to my imaginary new Bel Air home. But big-budget, high-profile, starring roles don't always turn out the way you imagine. Coppola's labor of love, which was supposed to be a low-budget $12 million movie, ended up costing more than $27 million to make. That was a whole lot back in 1981, particularly when the leads were only making $25,000 each. On the set we started calling it "One from the Purse," and at some point all the nonunion employees agreed to take only 50 percent of their salaries for an indefinite period of time. A few weeks later, Francis came to the set and made a speech to the cast and crew explaining that we were out of money and no one would be paid for two weeks. There was a long pause. Then someone finally spoke: "We're in. We'll stay." It was really touching that Francis got support from this seemingly hard-as-nails Hollywood film crew. They were on his side, and they loved him. The first assistant director got up and said, "Okay, Let's go. Back to work. Time is money." I looked at Freddy Forrest and said "No, time is just time now, isn't it?"

But in spite of the outpouring of loyalty for Francis, the investors pulled their funding during production, and Coppola ended up paying for much of the film himself. He confidentially screened the work-in-progress for theater owners, part of the process to lock in distribution plans. But the press must have infiltrated the private screenings because early negative reviews came out across the country. Paramount, the distributors, backed out. Zoetrope Studios collapsed. It was a disaster.

Everyone's eyes were on Francis, who had become something of a god after *The Godfather* and *Apocalypse Now*. There was just too much pressure on that one little film. The press built it up, then tore it down. After all the hoopla, all the parties and expectations, it made a much better story for the movie to fail. I suspect, to use a very twenty-first-century word that would never have caught on in the '80s, that there was a bit of schadenfreude going on, where certain people were taking a bit of pleasure in the movie's failure. I'll always wonder what would have happened if Zoetrope had survived and we'd continued on as the acting troupe that Francis envisioned.

I hadn't seen *One from the Heart* in years. Recently, when they released a DVD with a remixed soundtrack that takes advantage of advances in sound technology, I went to a screening at the Academy in Beverly Hills. After more than twenty years, I can say I'm proud of my work in the film. I didn't always feel that way. When the movie wasn't a hit, I felt responsible. I remember watching comedienne Kitty Carlisle come out of the premiere at Radio City Music Hall. A CBS reporter shoved a microphone in her face and asked what she thought. She said, "Awful, darling, just awful. What a waste of film." OUCH! But when I saw it at the Academy this time around, I knew it wasn't my fault that the movie had failed. It wasn't anybody's. We were a talented group, directed by a brilliant director. I loved it.

We all make sacrifices to do what we love. For me, dancing on the cement street of our Las Vegas set wasn't the worst of it. There's a scene in the opening of *One from the Heart* in which I get out of a car with a ton of groceries, then drop them all over the sidewalk. It sets the tone for my character, who is overwhelmed by her mundane life. After a couple of takes, Francis decided to try the scene another way, with a champagne bottle falling out of one of the bags and exploding on the pavement.

It was meant to foreshadow our anniversary celebration, which would explode into a fight. A prop guy grabbed a bottle of champagne from the prop truck, always the place to go for booze or anything illicit. It was a fine bottle of Moët, intended for our weekly Friday-night party on the lot. This was not a prop bottle, mind you, but a real, heavy, glass bottle of champagne. I dropped that bottle again and again until, finally, the pressure built up and the bottle exploded. A shard of glass sliced into the top of my foot, severing a tendon. At that moment, a grave warning signal went off in my head. It was beyond the pain of the injury. I just knew something strange had happened.

A number of people with MS believe they can trace the onset of the disease to a specific, physically traumatic moment in their lives. Most studies say that there is no scientific link between trauma and MS. Those scientists—they have no sense of drama. Rather, they say that the MS itself is probably the reason for the trauma in the first place—people with MS are more likely to find themselves falling or otherwise hurting themselves. Say what you will, I blame that champagne bottle.

I didn't rehearse for two weeks so that my foot could heal, and it did, enough so I could dance. The show must go on, right? But toward the end of filming, something started happening to me. My foot was healing, but my body was talking to me in ways it never had before. I didn't recover quite as well as I should have. I was overwhelmingly exhausted, and finishing the movie took everything out of me. My body just wasn't behaving normally.

At the time, I chalked it up to overwork. There it was—probably my first serious episode of multiple sclerosis—and I paid no attention. I figured everyone was as tired as I was. I thought it was the stress, the long hours, and the pressure I put on myself to be the best I could be in my biggest role to date. Maybe I shouldn't have dismissed what my body was telling me, but I didn't want to hear it back then.

That was fifteen years before I was told for the first time that I might have MS. My career was going so well. Kwitcher Bitchin', I thought to myself. It wouldn't be fair to Moët for me to hold that bottle of champagne responsible for my MS. But I really do believe that in that instant, when that glass cut my foot, something changed . . . for good.

11

My Marriage to Dave . . .

The physical exhaustion I felt during the filming of *One from the Heart* disappeared soon thereafter from my consciousness and my memory. I was busy filming *Tootsie*, one of the best roles of my career, and one I almost refused. Yes, siree, folks, you heard it here: I almost didn't do *Tootsie* because the role I was offered, that of Sandy Lester, wasn't the lead.

A couple of months after I finished *One from the Heart*, I heard about a new movie that Sydney Pollack was doing with Dustin Hoffman. Every actress in Hollywood was auditioning for *Tootsie*, but my agents couldn't land me an audition despite the fact that I'd just wrapped a starring role in Coppola's big new movie. Even my exercise teacher at Jane Fonda had an audition! But I couldn't get one. I was outraged. Then the great Elaine May did a rewrite of the script. I had once done a reading of one of her plays at the Phoenix Theatre in New York, and she must have liked what she saw because, apparently, when she turned in her version of the script, she told Sydney Pollack that Teri Garr was the only one who could play the role of Sandy.

Aha! Now the tables were turned, and they wanted me for the movie. But it wasn't even the lead role. As far as I was concerned, it was too little, too late. They'd have to do their little movie without me. Except . . . it was Sydney Pollack, a great, talented, and powerful director. So I agreed to have a meeting and talk about it. (Nice of Queen Teri, huh?)

On my way to the meeting with Sydney, I gave myself a pep talk. "I'm gonna play the game," said I to me. "But I'm really saying no. I'm trying to build a career here." I guess Sydney had anticipated my reluctance; before I could even begin to demur, he charmed me. He explained that Elaine May had championed me, and he admitted that he was persuading me for her sake. I appreciated his honesty. He was so straightforward and charismatic that I was curious to see what it would be like to be under his direction. And I liked the way he talked about my character. He wanted her to be more than just a put-upon girlfriend. He knew the movie would walk a tightrope through the feminism of the day (it would be released in 1981) and explained that he believed I could make Sandy a complex character—believable, funny, and just sympathetic enough, without making Dustin's character seem like a jerk.

Sydney was a straight shooter. The more I talked to him, the more I wanted the chance to work with him. Besides, he showed me some scenes from the script, including one in which Sandy had a line that cracked me up: "I had a wonderful time at your party. Do you have any Seconal?" Plus, really, was I going to say no? Here was my chance to make a movie with Dustin Hoffman and Sydney Pollack! So I squelched my inner diva, who had said she'd only accept the lead, and took what turned out to be one of the most rewarding roles of my life.

Whenever you have a major part in a movie, you get a director's chair with your name on it. It's a status thing. I'd been in movies where I'd had a chair for the last few years, and had grown accustomed to it. Sometimes a hardworking girl needs to sit down and take a break. Especially a working girl like me, who was more fatigued than she'd care to admit. The first day on the *Tootsie* set, I realized I didn't have a chair with my name on it, and so I had nowhere to sit. I wasn't going to say anything, but I guess my lip was sticking out pretty far because when Dustin said, "Where's your chair?" and I said, "I haven't got one." So he scribbled my name on a chair with chalk and said, "Here, sit here." That was his style. He tried to make everyone comfortable; Dustin is a real mensch. We began a friendship that would last many decades.

My character, Sandy, was a confused girl who felt like she always had to fight to be heard. All that rage was hard for me to get. Halfway through the film, Michael (Dustin's character) tells Sandy that he's in love with another woman. According to the script and Sydney's direction I was supposed to freak out, but I just didn't buy her anger. It was the middle of the feminist movement. I'd read all the books of the moment, by Betty Friedan and Germaine Greer and others like them, while I was developing Sandy's character. I thought she'd be hurt and self-hating more than she'd be mad. But Sydney didn't want Sandy to be too helpless and victimized; that wasn't what the movie was about. So Dustin kept taunting me, trying to enrage me, and then Sydney had us ad-lib until we got into an on-camera screaming match.

Much to my own surprise, I dug Sandy's rage right out of those

1. Broadway Babe Phyllis "Legs" Lind in the midthirties, around the time she met my dad.

2. Eddie Garr, early 1930s, vaudeville headliner.

3. The house where I lived in Lakewood, Ohio. My brothers and I shared the attic . . . the Anne Frank years.

4. Miss Teri Ann Garr, future water-bomb thrower.

5. Cleveland, Ohio, 19?? Dressed in babushka by Austrian relatives, attempting comedy in retaliation.

6. Phil, Ed, and me at Niagara Falls, 1950s. Had my hand on my heart in every picture that day, because the Customs man asked if we were all "Americans." Damn straight!

7. Unhappily on our way to another road trip cross-country.

8. The Huston Street gang, Sally, Linda, Teri, and Sharon, just after knocking over a liquor store.

9. Teri Garr, Ballerina Extraordinaire. Age ten.

10. A picture taken at Goldwyn Studios, at the audition for the film *West Side Story*. I was trying to look at least eighteen.

11. Sharon, Teri, Bob Banas our choreographer, Joanie, and Maruska. Dancers on the wonderful *Shivaree*. You remember that show, don't you? 1960s.

12. Hampton Fancher and me, 1968. Trying to appear aloof in one of our happiest moments.

13. Piazza San Marco, Venice, 1968. Filming an episode of *It Takes a Thief* with several of my fellow players.

14. Dancing with Annette Funicello in *Pajama Party*, 1969.

15. Happily dancing in North Hollywood Park, hoping to get discovered by Flo Ziegfeld, even though he was dead by then.

16. Harrison Ford and I visiting our manager, Pat McQueeny. Ford went on to do space movies, I think.

17. Teri on the roof, New York City, 1971. Nice pants.

18. My apartment in New York City. This is me "plantin' the back 40." The Hudson River is in the background.

19. Raul Julia, me, and Francis Coppola in Las Vegas, 1972. Rehearsing *One from the Heart*. Also, my birthday.

20. Jackie Gleason and Ms. Garr in *The Sting II*, 1973.

21. Me and the magician, Steve Martin, around 1975, doing *The Sonny and Cher Comedy Hour*. Don't know what ever became of him?

22. Sandy Rovetta, Cher, and Ms. Garr on *The Sonny and Cher Show*. My hair was interesting, but how about Cher's nails?

23. Publicity shot from *Young Frankenstein*. I'm wearing Julie Andrews' dress from *Star!*, backwards!

24. "Young Frankenstein"—Gene Wilder—and me, 1976.

25. Buck Henry and me dancing in the garden around 1976.

26. What can I say? With John Denver in *Oh, God!*

27. With Richard Dreyfuss in *Close Encounters of the Third Kind*, where God was revealed as a chandelier. Mobile, Alabama, 1977.

28. My home in Laurel Canyon. We called it the "Munchkin House" because the front door came up to my chin.

29. Roger and me in our yard in Laurel Canyon, 1981. He just found out I don't cook, clean, or do heavy lifting.

30. The kitchen in my Laurel Canyon house. "Special" dinners meant that you couldn't actually eat them . . . they were too special.

31. Future producer and hair model, Roger Birnbaum, and Ms. Garr around 1981 or so.

32. My friends, Henry Post and Andy Warhol, at Elaine's in New York City. Early eighties.

33. Dustin Hoffman, Ms. Garr, and Sydney Pollack, trying to direct us. Dustin wasn't buying.

34. Could this be where I actually caught MS?

35. Me in Hollywood, 1983. Farrah Fawcett loaned me her hair for this photo.

36. The film in which I played a woman tragically addicted to pancakes.

37. *Saturday Night Live* with Eddie Murphy and Joe Piscopo. I was going for a Diane Sawyer look, even though she was always copying me . . . even to this day!

38. Michael Keaton and me in *Mr. Mom*. We were doing a weird Zen exercise.

39. *Moi à* Paris *avec la Tour Eiffel. Très jolie,* 1985.

40. Being honored at the Santa Barbara Film Fest in 1987. Arriving with David Kipper, Buck Henry, and Tom Schiller, all of whom believed I was their date. Fun ensued.

41. David Kipper happily trying to strangle me in Mexico City, 1988.

42. Shirley MacLaine (my real mother in another life) and me on the set of *Waiting for the Light*, 1990.

43. Visiting the Bushes Sr. in 1990. I just informed George that we were having chicken nuggets for dinner. He was very excited. They are just simple people at heart.

44. At our wedding in Cabo San Lucas, Mexico, 1993. John just told me that his mom changed his sheets every day. Would I be doing that too, he wondered?

45. Brought Molly home to our rented house, and she started copying me immediately. She couldn't figure out that painting, either.

46. Molly—again trying to copy me, backyard, 1994.

47. Dragging Miss Molly to Paris in 1994 to shoot *Prêt à Porter* for Robert Altman. She seemed to think it was funny.

48. Christmas 1996 after Molly's first self-haircut. Very Jean Seberg, no?

49. Dragging Molly to work again. Everybody in our 'hood cruises around in limos wearing shades.

50. Tom Arnold, Jon Lovitz, me, and Nancy Davis at the Race to Erase MS event, 2002.

51. "Mophead," as Molly was called at Mammoth's Carnival Days. She made it out of table napkins.

52. Learning the ropes of ski racing: Show the logo and give 'em a big smile.

feminist books and burst out, "I never said 'I love you'! I don't care about 'I love you.' I read *The Second Sex*! I read *The Cinderella Complex*! I'm responsible for my own orgasms. I don't care. I just don't like to be lied to!"

Everybody liked it, including Sydney, and I was completely spent.

During *Tootsie* I remember really wanting to lose five pounds. What actress doesn't, right? But maybe I have Owen Roizman, the director of photography, who's also known for shooting *The French Connection, The Exorcist,* and many other films, to thank. He admitted in a press interview with Susan Dworkin for *Ms.* that after the first day of filming, Dustin and Sydney looked at the dailies—the film that had been shot that day—and said that Owen had made me look too pretty. After that, he tried to "compromise a little bit and just try to make [me] look decent."

Well, when I got my look at the dailies, I didn't like what I saw. "Decent" wasn't good enough for me, but rather than blame it on the photography, I blamed it on my weight.

Dustin Hoffman, bless his heart, always had a solution to every problem. When I asked him how to drop some weight, he gave me two pieces of advice: Snack on fresh fruit, and sit in the sauna. How eighties is that? Dustin told me that Paul Newman used a sauna to lose weight, so that sealed the deal. (I love Paul Newman.) Every day after we got off the set I went to the gym to sit and sweat. It was like a game. I was so determined to lose those five pounds, I challenged myself to see how long I could last, starting with ten minutes, increasing to half an hour, then finally making it a full forty-five minutes. Then I would drag myself out of there, drained beyond belief, thinking I was doing something good for myself. After all, when I came out of the sauna I was a good pound or two lighter than I'd been when I went in—at least until I drank a glass of water. The sauna made me so weak I could barely walk, but I told myself that was normal. It was business as usual. I didn't know how to be any other way. Today I know that the absolute worst thing for MS is heat. But at the time it appeared to be a brilliant weight-loss plan.

Tootsie was a hit. As Vincent Canby observed in the *New York Times,* Pollack and the writers had "taken a wildly improbable situation and found just about all of its comic possibilities, not by exaggerating the obvious, but by treating it with inspired common sense." People couldn't get enough of the role reversal, and I was thrilled to be a part of it. Even my mother, who was still doing what she had always done—working on the NBC shows and living in Burbank—had to admit that things were going pretty well for me. She sent me clippings of the reviews with every bit that mentioned me underlined. She always especially liked the interviews in which I mentioned that she'd been a Rockette.

And then, of course, there were the Academy Awards. I felt like a pro, and from the outside it may have looked like I breezed onto the silver screen goofy, windswept, and blond. But now you know I'd paid my dues. Yes, I *was* goofy, windswept, and blond. But the appearance of breeziness was the real performance that should have won me an Oscar.

I rode high all through the Academy Awards, appreciating my success all the more for how hard I'd worked for it, and for how much it would have meant to my dad. I can't imagine anything making him happier. His life had been a lost gamble, but what he never lost was the conviction that he was talented and that he was supposed to be successful. Although my tactics were different—I didn't rely on luck—I was proof that even though our family wasn't *Ozzie and Harriet,* we had what it took to make it in showbiz.

The joyride of the Oscars didn't last long. The next day, I was right back to work, filming *Mr. Mom,* the title of which I was campaigning unsuccessfully to change to *Mr. Mom and Mrs. Dad.* But the memory of that night lingered, a bit of unassailable success that I kept like a charm in my back pocket.

Mr. Mom starred the delightful Michael Keaton as a family man who's just lost his job. I played his wife, who becomes a successful ad executive. My character uses her maternal knowledge to come up with the winning ad campaign—"Schooner Tuna: The Tuna with a Heart"—for the agency's most important client and, since this was the movies, promotions, praise, and bonuses ensue. My character takes it too far, becoming a workaholic and eventually realizing what she misses about mothering. But the movie doesn't sell her out; in the end she and her husband find compromises that make the family work without requiring them to return to the typical gender roles, not like in life. I did what I could to make that character a bit more complex; when she had to leave her kids on Halloween to go work, for instance, I insisted that it be hard for her. Halloween's a big night for a family! What working mother wouldn't look mournfully behind at her little goblins and ghosts as she got called away on business? Of course, I can't say that my own working mother gave it a second thought, but I guess she could argue that with me playing Ginger Rogers in her wardrobe room, every day was Halloween.

Mercifully, I was so busy with *Mr. Mom* that I didn't have even time to watch TV to see what the post-Oscars coverage said about my dress/football uniform. When I look back, I see that that was the story of my life. I was too busy to think, talk, hang out. Too busy to gab with friends about who we were dating or what to wear. Too busy to do anything but work on the next movie, read the next script, prepare for the next role. After the way I grew up, it was hard for me to feel secure with what I'd already achieved. I had to be confident, in the words of Scarlett O'Hara, that I'd never go hungry again.

Even for a girl who couldn't kick back, those years were pretty great. I was working with Francis Ford Coppola, Martin Scorsese, Robert Altman, Sydney Pollack, Steven Spielberg, and, of course, the very funny Mel Brooks. I also started doing the talk-show circuits more frequently after my *Tootsie* nomination.

I first met David Letterman when I was doing a promotional tour for *Young Frankenstein* in 1974. Twentieth Century Fox sent me to ten cities in ten days. As part of the tour, I was a guest on the Indianapolis radio show Dave was hosting at the time. We hit it off right away. Eventually, he got his own show on NBC, at 12:30, after Johnny Carson. That was *Late Night with David Letterman*. In the early '80s I went on that show every chance I got. Sometimes it was planned, sometimes—not so much. Often, I would get a call from Robert (Morty) Morton, Dave's producer at the time, asking if I could be in New York for the next night's show. I always asked, "Who died?" and then hopped on a plane, anyway. At first I did it to promote the movies I was in, but my rapport with Dave grew, I just did it for fun. And I mean fun in the masochistic sense of the word. Dave reminded me of my older brothers; he was always trying to get my goat, and he usually succeeded. Every time I went on the show I wound up exasperated. He'd make fun of me for being "ill prepared," or he'd goad me into telling some story—like my story about going to the party at Elvis's—when I had no desire to tell it. I'd toss my hair and threaten to storm off the stage, but then I'd stay for the abuse and come back for more. (It wasn't really abuse, it was comedy. There's a fine line.) I guess what it comes down to is that I was happy to entertain, even if it was at my own expense. I liked being in front of the live studio audience. That immediacy, the same immediacy I'd gotten used to on *Sonny and Cher*, was missing in the movie world.

One November night in 1985 Dave decided to do a show from his office. Not the studio, mind you, but his actual office, upstairs from the studio. It was the "Too Tired to Do a Show" show. I was the first guest to appear that night. We sat in his office. There was no audience, so there was no laughter, live or canned. He said, "This is my office. I have my own bathroom. Do you want to see it? Do you want to take a shower?"

Did I smell bad? Was my hair oily? Was he nuts? Oh yeah, he was, and so was I. I told him I had no need for a shower. He asked again. And again. He must have asked me twenty-five times. When I was little my brothers would browbeat me like that. They'd say, "Go drop this soda off the roof." I'd refuse, but they'd keep at it until I caved. I had the same dynamic with Dave, and I knew he wouldn't shut up about the shower until I relented. "Okay, fine." I got in the shower, closed the door, stripped down to my underpants, and turned on the water. Dave had won. He'd beaten me down, and across America every guy who'd ever tried to talk a girl into doing something she didn't want to do must have felt a small sense of victory. I thought of it as locker-room humor. We continued to have a conversation while I showered. We were shouting back and forth; the water was on; the mike was wet. I know it sounds tame now, but in those days it was as scandalous as Janet Jackson flashing her breast during the Super Bowl. The last words you heard as the show ended were from me, yelling over the shower: "I hate you, Dave!" After the show I walked home to my apartment, thirty blocks in soaking-wet underwear. Yes, I walked. I always refused the limos they offered; I thought of myself as too down-to-earth for limos. Except this time I was walking home with damp drawers and wondering if this if how Katharine Hepburn had started.

Anything for Dave.

Once you're on TV, you're in the public domain, and people feel that they can say anything to you. A few weeks later as I was walking through O'Hare International Airport in Chicago, a man came up to me and said, "You and Dave are having a thing, right?" I said, "No." He said, "Well, I ran into Dave last week, and he said you were." From then on, when people asked if we were having a thing, I'd say, "Yes, a big, big affair, if it's any of your business. And I'm not sure that it is." The truth was that occasionally Dave would call, but our relationship was mostly on-camera. Except for the seven years we were married.

In addition to doing Letterman's show, I did *The Tonight Show with Johnny Carson* a lot. My dialogue with Dave was always a bit antagonistic, so I always felt like I was on the defensive. But with Johnny I felt safe. He made me feel comfortable and at home. And what I loved most about Johnny was that between the stars, authors, and experts, he always had quirky regular people on the show. One time I was on with an eighty-year-old woman from the Midwest who was a skilled canner. She showed Johnny some of the foods she had canned, and she spoke candidly, pardon the pun, with him about her craft. She told him, "People are always trying to put *me* in a can. They say you *should* get married, you *should* have kids. Well, Johnny, marriage and kids are just a few of the cans I'm not gonna get into." I loved how self-assured and independent she was. Johnny truly relished characters like her. He clearly understood that their lives were as interesting and important as those of the stars who came there to plug their big movies.

Johnny really set me straight once. In 1984, I got talked into singing the opening number at the Academy Awards. Stanley Donen, who directed *Singin' in the Rain,* had conceived an idea for a takeoff on *Flying Down to Rio,* an old Ginger Rogers movie. A 747 would actually be brought onstage for the number, and I was supposed to be atop the wing, hanging on for dear life. There would be a quick cut to Ginger, tied to the wing of a biplane, then a cut to me waving onstage, then a cut to King Kong on the Empire State Building, waving, and then back to me again. Then, I was supposed to do some kicks or turns or something. While all of this was going on, boy dancers would prance out carrying suitcases, quickly rip off my skirt, and replace it with feathers. Very Vegas, circa '57.

I wasn't totally sold on the idea but, hey, this was Stanley Donen. He really, really wanted me to do it, and he was a friend, so I did him a favor. How bad could it be?

The day of the show, I went, as planned, to the Dorothy Chandler Pavilion. Immediately, I noticed that someone had waxed the stage to a shiny gloss. I thought, how the hell am I going to dance on this? So I raised my hand and yelled up to the booth, "Hey, somebody waxed the floor. Can anybody fix this?" Nothing. Nada. There was all this hustling and excitement going on, and I was being totally ignored.

I went into my dressing room and waited like I was on death row. Finally, I heard the show starting and prepared to meet my fate. Out on the stage, I began the number. What choice did I have?

Next thing I knew, I was slipping and sliding all over the place.

I thought, Jesus, Mary, and Joseph, can I just disappear? I looked out into the audience. There's Jack Nicholson. There's Milos Forman, who'd directed *The Loves of a Blonde*. I can't believe I was up there thinking of résumés when I was supposed to be entertaining 500 million people on TV. And yet, as horrible as it was, I was holding it together. And then I looked out and saw Sam Shepard and (the insufferable) Jessica Lange staring smugly back at me.

So, what does this have to do with Johnny Carson, you might ask? Well, I was supposed to be on his show the next day, and once the *Los Angeles Times* said the opening number on the Academy Awards was a disaster, I was totally humiliated. (They also said that "If a brick could sing, it would sound like Teri Garr.") So, given this, I decided that for once I would follow my instincts and cancel my appearance on *The Tonight Show*.

Half an hour after I called in sick to the show, the woman who usually booked me called back. I told her about the review, and an hour later, Johnny Carson himself called me.

I think he hardly ever called anybody. I'll admit I was a little intimidated. But I told Johnny the whole story. "First," he said, "Remember this . . . no favor goes unpunished." Then he said, "So what if you got a bad review? You know how many bad reviews I've had? You just keep going. Don't let anybody stop you. It doesn't matter in the great scheme of things what they think. They don't know anything."

There was something very showbiz familial about this advice. It was pretty similar to what my own damn family had been pounding in my head for as long as I could remember.

After talking to Johnny, I went on the show, and it was great.

Things are different now. A year later, Rob Lowe did the opening number at the Academy Awards. He sang "Proud Mary" with Snow White and Minnie Mouse, and it completely obliterated any bad taste I had left over from my performance. It was at least fifty times worse than my airport extravaganza. So, hey, Rob, here's to you, babe. I owe you one.

When I was doing my nighttime talk-show hopping, I was still living up on Lookout Mountain with Roger Birnbaum. Roger had been my boyfriend since 1979, a couple years before I did *Tootsie*. We met when I lived in an apartment on Sunset Plaza Drive in the Hollywood Hills. I was glad when my next-door neighbor moved out—his late-night sexual gymnastics kept waking me up. Then I met Roger at the mailboxes and found out that he'd moved in next door. He was cute, tall, and slender with dark, curly hair, and the only sounds that came from his apartment were the cheers of guys watching basketball. It was a real improvement. We became friends, and it was like living a sitcom. Day and night we'd knock on each other's windows and doors. Then one weekend I had overnight guests, so I stayed in his apartment. He had worked for the music producer Clive Davis and had great taste in music. This was before I shot *One from the Heart,* and he introduced me to— or should I say seduced me with—Tom Waits. By the time my guests left my apartment, I wasn't just sleeping at Roger's for the convenience.

When we first started dating, we tried to break through the wall from his apartment to mine. Our bedrooms seemed to share a wall, so we took a hammer and tried to bang out a hole connecting the bedrooms, but when we broke through his wall it came through the back of my closet, which wasn't quite as festive. At best, I could use the hole as a laundry chute. Finally, I literally moved next door, into his apartment. He was adorable, nice, funny, smart, and tenacious, and we were really tight. I loved that his approach to life was different from mine. He had strong tastes—in art, music, food, everything. When he saw a beautiful, simple landscape by Jim Ganzer (who collaborated with Ed Ruscha) he said, "This is good. Let's buy it." We'd drive down the coast and he'd say, "See that shack? A guy can sit down there and have a cold beer and a cracked crab." I was always impressed that he knew what he liked and where to find it. Roger was sophisticated. He knew how to tap into what was already there (even though he was from New Jersey).

Roger also had a laid-back love of life that was refreshing. We were always throwing parties and barbecues. The first summer we dated, we had a party for my birthday I'll never forget. Penny Marshall was there, as were producer Sean Daniel, who'd go on to produce many movies; Freddy Forrest, my costar in *One from the Heart;* Sean Daniel's girlfriend Linda Marder; and Alfa-Betty and Marshall. I cooked hamburgers for hours as an endless stream of people poured in bearing six-packs. Except my dear friend Toni— she always came empty-handed, or with some feathers or something. Kevin Kline sat and played the piano for hours, and he was great.

I had told Roger that when I was a kid sometimes I didn't get a birthday cake, that my mother would just bring me a Hostess Cupcake with a candle in it. Roger surprised me with a cake he'd ordered. It was made to look like a huge Hostess Cupcake, complete with that squiggle of white icing on the top.

In 1982, right after John Belushi died, a group of us decided to charter our own pleasure cruise to Catalina, an island about an hour off the coast. We were a motley crew, including me and

Roger, *SNL* writer Michael O'Donoghue, his girlfriend Carol Caldwell, Carrie Fisher (my actress friend who was most famous at the time for her performance as Princess Leia in *Star Wars*), and *SNL* writer and performer Albert Brooks, who would go on to write and perform in countless brilliant movies. It was a big sailboat with two staterooms and a huge refrigerator of booze. Chaos ensued. As we approached Catalina, our friendly captain informed us that we were in the cove where Natalie Wood had died the year before. Carol and I drunkenly jerry-rigged a Ouija board in order to contact the ghost of Natalie Wood. But when our pointer started moving around the letter board, the ghost who revealed himself was none other than John Belushi. Carol insisted she wasn't moving the pointer, and I most certainly wasn't moving it, so it had to be John Belushi, right? He told us that there was a conspiracy in L.A. involving then chief of police Daryl Gates and a prostitution ring. Carol and I briefly contemplated whether it was our civic duty to turn in Gates based on Belushi's testimony, but we were interrupted by a sound from the end of the boat. Albert had found a bullhorn and was shouting things like, "The makeup boat will be here in five minutes . . . All those needing makeup or wigs, please stand on deck." But it wasn't all fun and games. There were quizzes on Hollywood credits. I think we were trying to emulate that glamorous Hollywood lifestyle of the '30s and '40s. I think we failed, but we had fun trying.

Under his laid-back charm, Roger was a go-getter. He knew how to conserve his energy for the important stuff. I was impressed by his knack for the business. Sometimes I'd wake up in the middle of the night and find him missing from the bed. I'd discover him in the dark living room, reading scripts under the dim lamp. If Roger had scripts to read, he'd stay up all night to do it. If there was a director he wanted to meet, he'd make it happen. He'd pick someone out of a crowd, such as then Paramount producer Jeffrey Katzenberg or spouses and producing partners Lucy Fisher and Doug Wick, and end up in a conversation with them. We'd go out to dinner with Henry Winkler, who by then had his own production company at Paramount, and his wife Stacey at a fish place on Pico called Hymie's Fish Market. There'd be four other people in our party, and I'd know that they were important people, but for the life of me I couldn't remember who they were. I'm sure Roger still knows everyone we ate dinner with at Hymie's. That networking always felt like work to me, but it was effortless for him. He felt comfortable and natural doing it.

Roger was one of my great teachers. He was ambitious and driven, and at the same time completely true to himself and centered about his career. He seemed to have the attitude, I'm going to take what is rightfully mine. Eventually, we were spending so much time together that we decided to buy a house. We found a little cottage in Laurel Canyon, on Lookout Mountain. It was originally built as a set for Westerns in the '20s. How apropos, living in a movie set. It looked like a big house from the street, but it had been built to three-quarters perspective for the movies, so when I got up close to the door, it only came up to my nose. Anyway, we lived in the munchkin house, and that's when I filmed *Tootsie*.

My house was shrunken and my movie career was larger than life, but my relationship with Roger was real. I was comfortable and happy with him, and having a true companion helped keep everything else in perspective. For a while.

12

Tripped Up

Soon after *Tootsie*, the Academy Awards, and magical weight-loss saunas draining all the sense from my body, Roger and I started wearing thin. It was 1983. We'd been together for five years. When I try to figure out how and why it happened, the most I can come up with is that we were young and foolish. Okay, maybe I was younger and more foolish than he was. He'd want to go fishing with his buddies, and I'd get jealous that I couldn't go. I was clingy and mad that he wanted to have a life without me. Roger was nice about it but couldn't understand why I was like that. Neither could I, really. Then I was off to Europe to do an HBO made-for-TV movie called *To Catch a King* with Robert Wagner, and Roger wasn't thrilled that I was in Portugal having lobster on the beach with Robert Wagner. Show-business relationships are difficult. All relationships are difficult.

I had started getting used to being admired from afar. My

movies were popular. I was getting fan mail. People were coming up to me in the supermarket to say, "You're Teri Garr, I love you." They thought they knew me but, of course, they didn't. But unlike a real relationship, which required me to give of myself, I didn't have to give anything to get their attention.

I didn't realize it then, but (thank you, therapy) on some level I thought at the time that the public attention was enough. It kept me safe and protected, an arm's length away. In a way, I wasn't reared to hope for any greater love than that. I dumped many a decent boyfriend because of that subconscious belief. I think of the phrase, "You can't hit a moving target," and I think of myself. I just kept moving; those were such busy years. There was no time to think. I'd fly here, fly there, do *Letterman,* do *The Tonight Show,* wake up, start all over.

I barely saw my friends. But then everybody was busy. I was grateful for my friend Heidi Schaeffer, who worked for PMK. Whenever I did a big studio movie, PMK would set me up on the talk shows, and Heidi was assigned to accompany me. We struck up a friendship, and after she helped me clean out my closet—the greatest of all bonding experiences—we became friends for life.

When I wasn't in New York, I'd trade messages with Alfa-Betty and Marshall on our answering machines for months, and that's how it was with almost everyone. My friendships were in maintenance mode. My house was a place to repack my suitcase. There were no leisurely Sunday barbecues or walks on the beach. There was no time to make my bed, to arrange flowers, to read the news, or even see what Bruce Springsteen was up to. All the things that are important in life.

After I shot the HBO movie with Robert Wagner I went to Paris. I was more interested in having fun and pushing my career than in returning home to my life with Roger, and he could tell. When I came back from Europe we officially broke up. I bought Roger out of the munchkin house. When we divided up the books and music, a cloud crossed over our years together. All my photos from the Oscars showed him smiling beside me. Thank-you notes addressed to the two of us slid out of books. Our lives had become more intertwined than I had realized. I knew exactly what kind of music we had liked to hear when we woke up in the morning. All the familiar things were going to be gone. We said good-bye in the driveway, both of us crying. It was sad and difficult.

I fled to New York.

At the time, I had an apartment on West Eleventh Street in New York City. My old friends Marshall and Alfa-Betty lived there, and when Alfa-Betty had called me a few years back to tell me that there was an empty apartment two floors below them, I'd snatched it up. It was a great building—a woman wearing a hair net sat at the switchboard in the lobby and took packages and mail. She'd say, "Your book has arrived," and hand me a magazine. I liked that she called magazines books. And I loved that little apartment. It had a bedroom with two windows that the sun poured through, and my closet was painted yellow. The kitchen ran across one wall of the only other room, like in *The Honeymooners*. It was a cheery, charming place in the Village.

Whenever I came to town I'd call up Marshall and Alfa-Betty and we'd walk over to Il Cantinori, a wonderful Tuscan restaurant on East Tenth Street, for long, wine-filled dinners. Marshall would feed me ideas for what to talk about on *Letterman*. He'd say, "When he asks you about relationships, tell him you're dating Boris Yeltsin," or whatever else came into his head. He claims I never used any of it, but I'm pretty sure I declared my love for

Boris Yeltsin on national television at least once. On the way home from dinner, Marshall and I would collect "found art" on the streets to decorate our apartments. He would scream out, "Good trash, good trash," and the bargaining would begin. We fought for several blocks over a Good Humor ice-cream sign—not very good-humored of us. Marshall won, but he promises he's leaving me that sign in his will. My lifestyle in New York was very mature.

When I wasn't in town I would sublet the apartment to my old friend Griffin Dunne. It was an illegal sublet, so we told the landlords that Griffin and I were boyfriend and girlfriend. When they started to get suspicious, Griffin would say, "Time to stage a fight in the lobby to prove we're in love. Get ready." We were crazy about that apartment, and we were willing to use our thespian talents to prove it. I'd come in from Los Angeles and swoop into the lobby at a prearranged time. It was showtime. We'd stage a huge domestic argument. I would scream, "Honey, it just isn't working." He would try to calm me down. Then we'd go up to the apartment and laugh. That would keep our scam going for another eight months, until we had to do it again. It worked for seven years. It might have been the best relationship with a man I ever had.

Around that time, Griffin had fallen in love with a script by Joseph Minion, a Columbia University student who had written it for a class. It was a dark comedy called *After Hours*. He always said that if he could find a way to get it made, he wanted me in it. Somehow Griffin not only managed to get it made, he convinced Martin Scorsese to direct. I loved that script. I played a lonely, Monkee-obsessed waitress with an anachronistic beehive. It was a clever, Kafkaesque tale of New York at night.

Starting a week before the shoot, Martin wanted me to come to his Tribeca loft every day for lunch so he could "see what I was like." I was nervous before the first meeting. I had no idea what he was after. All I knew was if he wanted me to come over there and put an ice-cream cone on my head every day, I'd do it. That was my dancer's mentality. The director was the artist, and I respected that. Martin showed me into his loft and led me to a room that was wall-to-wall videotapes. There were film noir posters on the walls. I was impressed by his filmic knowledge, but after all, he *was* a film professor at NYU. I wanted to connect with him, but all I could manage to get out was, "I knew Truffaut." He wasn't impressed. All he wanted to talk about was the woman I was playing in *After Hours,* how I thought she was crazy, and how I thought I was crazy. Oh, fine.

We filmed *After Hours* entirely at night. We'd start work at around five o'clock and go until sunrise the next morning. Griffin played the lead, and Linda Fiorentino, Rosanna Arquette, Catherine O'Hara, and I played women he encountered over the course of a single strange night.

My character, Julie, lived in a loft on the third floor of a run-down SoHo building. Her bed was surrounded with mousetraps (a nice touch from the screenwriter). There was one scene in the movie where Julie was scripted to say, "I don't know what I've done with my brains . . . Where are my brains?" Then I would open up the refrigerator and there'd be clear plastic containers full of calf brains. I thought it was a joke—that she thought eating brains would make her smarter. But Martin seemed to want more from it. He kept saying "Do it again. Make her more frantic. Make her more hysterical." We must have done that scene fifty times, and I never got it right. I still feel bad about it. I just couldn't do it to Martin's satisfaction. The scene was ultimately cut from the movie, but it lingered in my guilt file.

I wanted to make it up to Martin. So one night I suggested that when I opened up my kitchen cupboard it should be chock-full of cans of Aquanet hairspray. Thankfully, he ended up using that, so my failure with the cow-brains scene was somewhat redeemed.

Martin was so careful with his actors. We were treated like royalty. He never let us become bothered or distracted. One rainy night Robert De Niro came to the set. I was filming a scene where I was just walking down the street, no big deal, and I asked if I could meet De Niro. Martin said "Oh, no, no, no, you stay in character." It wasn't so hard for me to stay in character; she was nuts and funny. Enough said.

Something changed for me in New York. I was at the top of my game. Years of hustling and hard work were finally paying off, and I was grateful for it. I had the life I'd always dreamed of living. I was young, independent, and successful. I should have been enjoying the ride. But that summer in New York was the start of my tripping years. I first noticed it when I was running. I was an avid jogger and loved running through Central Park. But at times my body felt weird to me. I couldn't quite put my finger on what was wrong—it was just off somehow. Now and then an odd feeling would come over me. The best way I can describe it is to say that my body felt lazy while my mind didn't. Sometimes I would take a day off from running, and sometimes I would ignore it and push myself even harder.

And then one day I tripped. I was running along, minding my own business, when suddenly I hurtled forward and nearly fell on my face. I looked around to curse the trickster who'd stuck his foot out in front of me, but there was no one in sight. I brushed the pebbles off my hands and didn't give it a second thought. Who doesn't stumble every once in a while?

But then it started happening more frequently. I'd be walking down the hallway toward the elevator when I'd trip on a nonexistent tree root. A tree root in a hallway? Hmm. There is a dancer's myth that says the more you trip, the better a dancer you are. So as I saw it, I had become a spectacular dancer. Still, I brushed all the tripping aside, reasoning that it was normal. But three or four times a day?

The tripping was the first in a series of strange symptoms that neither I nor my many doctors would put together as MS until much, much later. Soon after the tripping began I started to feel the ringing. Yes, ringing. And this was way before cell phones. (Well, we had cell phones, but they were the size of canoes.) The feeling was like a cell phone on vibrate that had been implanted in my right foot. Zzzzzzzzz! However annoying, I wasn't terribly concerned about it until during one particular run, when my right arm started tingling. It felt like a knife was stabbing me in the arm. But then, I was in Central Park, so maybe it *was* a knife. But as this chorus of tingling, tripping, beeping, and stabbing reached a crescendo, I couldn't ignore my symptoms anymore. My body was a discordant symphony, and I was definitely not the conductor.

As soon as we finished shooting *After Hours*, I sought medical advice. The first doctor I saw was an orthopedic surgeon who had an office on Central Park West. He spoke with a charming Irish brogue that made me want to follow every instruction that came out of his mouth. Unfortunately, what came out was, "We'll operate on Thursday!" Apparently, he thought my spine needed replacing or something. I joked, "Sorry, I'm closed on Thursdays, ha-ha," but I was genuinely shocked. I decided it might be a good idea to run this "operation" by my brother, Ed, who was an orthopedic surgeon in Southern California.

Ed was skeptical. He spoke to the Irish doctor on the phone and then called me back to say, "Nice accent, but it's time for a second opinion." Actually, what he really said was, "Are you nuts?! Get yourself straight to a neurologist." So I did.

Before long I had seen at least twenty doctors of all sorts—short/tall, bald/hairy, fat/thin, middle-aged/middle-aged, white/white, male/male . . . okay, they all shared some characteristics, but they all had different opinions. I conscientiously consulted my Screen Actors Guild health insurance and went to see their neurologist. By this time, the tingling, tripping, and beeping were entertaining me full-time. I was a mess. After a thorough exam the neurologist told me, with a great degree of authority, that I had a degenerative nerve disease of the spine. He believed that nerves were pressing against my spinal cord, causing all the noise and commotion in my body.

According to the doctor, there were two treatments for this condition. The first was Valium—lots of it. And the second was some weird rope, pulley, and sandbag contraption that looked like a medieval torture device.

Dr. Valium, as I fondly called him, started me on his namesake drug. He prescribed eighteen tons of Valium for ten days. That's more than a ton a day. Needless to say, I spent that time in the hospital, drugged beyond consciousness. But at the time I was in a total panic, if one can be panicked on that much Valium. I was supposed to start shooting *Firstborn*, a movie that, of last count, eight people have seen. The gossip columns reported that I was in the hospital. Even *People* magazine ran an article saying, "Getting into shape for a role can be debilitating. Just ask Teri Garr, who's now filming *Firstborn,* in which she plays a sensuous divorced mother. To look her sexy best for the movie, Garr began working out with weights. Whether that was the cause she's not sure, but she soon came up with a neck injury and spent several days in traction at a New York hospital."

How could I recover from my drug-induced trance in time to do the job? I wasn't worried about my health or my future well-being. Instead, I was embarrassed about how tired I was, and afraid I'd lose the job. When the press reported my hospitalization, Dustin Hoffman sent me flowers with a note saying, "I know this has something to do with sex." I wished.

When I was released from the hospital, Dr. Valium started me on phase two of the treatment—the at-home medieval torture device. I was supposed to strap the rope over a door with the pulleys and sandbags hanging on one side, and me, with the rope around my neck, on the other side. I was to do this for fifteen minutes twice a day to relieve the pressure on my spine. It was like having my very own home stretching rack; I could have hung myself if I'd been so inclined. I must have been desperate because I actually did it . . . stretch my neck, that is. Friends would come up to my apartment and say, "What the hell are you doing?" and I'd say, "I'm working on my next role as a giraffe, what do you think?" But at that point, I was scared, confused, and desperate to get better quickly, so I followed the doctor's orders. Besides, I really believed it was working. Call it the placebo effect, but the beeping and tingling seemed to be letting up. Plus, I'd grown seven inches.

Only later would I learn that the natural course of MS is to relapse and remit. My symptoms probably were receding on their own. I'm pretty sure it had nothing to do with the pulleys and sandbags.

Some of the endless parade of doctors were brilliant; some of them were busy thinking about their next yacht race. Others—the ones who really made my blood boil—wrote me off as a whiny star. I will never forget one highly recommended doctor on Fifth Avenue in New York City. After a chest X-ray and a few other "reflex" tests, he sat me down in his office and, in the most condescending manner imaginable, said, "What do I have to do to convince you that there is nothing wrong with you?" If I ever see him again, I'm going to show him my leg brace and then kick him in the shin with it. But not because I'm into revenge; just call it an educational gesture.

MS is a sneaky disease. Like some of my boyfriends, it has a tendency to show up at the most awkward times and then to disappear entirely. It would take more than twenty years for doctors to even figure out what was wrong with me. But I was used to challenges. It had been no cakewalk getting to where I was. In all that time of trying to figure out what was happening to my body—spinal taps, X-rays, strength and reflex tests, and countless other fancy procedures—many of the doctors made me feel like they knew my body better than I did. Those male authority figures—what was a girl to think? They acted like I was trying to get attention. But I wasn't faking it or hallucinating. And I wasn't having nervous breakdowns, and I sure didn't want that kind of attention.

My problems came and went because that's what MS does. An exacerbation is often followed by a quiet period—a remission—that can last months or years. MS is a tricky disease. I was young, I knew nothing about medicine, and I wanted to believe them when they told me I was fine. After all, I had a life to live, a career to manage, and a head full of dreams—I wanted better roles, a long-term relationship, and, someday, a family. I wanted a lot. It was hard enough to imagine balancing my career with a home life. It never crossed my mind that my next decade would be spent not just juggling doctor visits and movie shoots, but simply trying to balance on my own two feet.

13

Something Up My Butt

The late eighties were a blur of traveling around the world, film-ing *Miracles, Pack of Lies, Full Moon in Blue Water, Out Cold,* and *Let It Ride,* going to ever more disappointing doctors, trying to have a serious relationship, and picking up my dry cleaning. (Not necessarily in order of importance—if they were, I might have started with the dry cleaning. The dry cleaner was becoming my best friend. He was always glad to see me, and I tried to pre-tend that it was more about me than about the salad-dressing stain on my blouse. I wonder if he still has that shop on Rothdell Trail, on the first floor of Jim Morrison's old house, and if he still has my signed headshot up on the wall. I still have his.)

I was still living in Laurel Canyon with the ghosts of the '70s rock and rollers. When Carrie Fisher was married to Paul Simon, she lived next door to me, in a cabin that had been built as a movie set. They also had an amazing apartment in New York, but they stayed in the cabin when they were in L.A. It was a one-room affair with a hitching post in the front yard and a huge plastic cow in the back. Carrie would have cooking parties at her house. She'd hire a chef to give us a lesson, and we'd all watch him cook and try to learn how, but mostly we'd just drink a lot of wine. One October night Carrie pulled me over to a handsome man with curly hair and a great smile. She introduced him as Dr. David Kipper and told him it was my birthday. It wasn't even close to my birthday, and even if it had been I never would have mentioned it. Anyway, a few days later I was jogging in my neighborhood, on Mulholland Drive, when David drove up to me and tooted his car horn. He rolled down his window and said, "Remember me?" I said, "Sure. It's still not my birthday." He lived in my neighborhood, and from then on he'd stop and chat whenever he saw me jogging, but he thought I was still dating Roger.

The next winter when I came down with strep, someone told me to go see this David Kipper, who was supposed to be a very good doctor. He gave me antibiotics, and when he handed me the prescription, he asked me again if Roger was still in the picture. When the answer was no, he wrote out a second prescription— this one for a lunch date with him. As soon as I was feeling better, we met for lunch near his office, at the Hamburger Hamlet on Sunset Boulevard (Hello, Norma Desmond). He was charming, good-looking, and unattached. And then he started leaving little notes in my mailbox. I'd come out in the morning and find a slip of paper that read, "Have a nice day," or "Do your calves need massaging?" He was sweet, so I went for it.

When David and I started dating, I was already spending half my free time seeing doctors about my leg. My mother was in complete denial about that, but she loved that I was dating a doctor. All my other boyfriends, with the exception of Roger, had been . . . well, hooligans. When my family finally met David, they loved him, too. I was delighted to be with someone who wasn't in show business. He was attentive and gentlemanly, always bringing peonies or other flowers I liked when he took me out to dinner. And he seemed to love buying me presents. If I mentioned a coat that I liked at Neiman Marcus, he'd show up with it the next day. It got so that I'd say, "I like purple cashmere sweaters," knowing that one would magically appear. Every present came with a greeting card. In his neat, all-caps handwriting (so un-doctorly!), David would create a crossword puzzle just for me, or simply remind me that he loved me.

David did his best to work around my career, flying to visit me on movie sets whenever he could. Once we went to Hawaii so I could shoot a Pepsi commercial. After my work was done, we went to stay in a fancy hotel on Maui. Biking to the beach, we passed a guy who offered to sell us pot. We rode past him nonchalantly, but once we got to the beach we changed our minds. I sent David back to buy a joint from him. The tabloids weren't the unrelenting presence that they are today, but I still didn't want to be recognized as a poster child for marijuana. So David rode back alone and bought a joint from the guy. But just as he was leaving the guy took another look at him and said, "Hey, you're the guy who was with Teri Garr." So much for anonymity.

From the very beginning of our relationship, David started saying he was crazy about me. It was a little overwhelming. I thought he was moving too fast, and there was something about his single-mindedness that I didn't entirely trust. Then, when he and I had only been dating about eight months, he came over to pick me up for dinner one night and gave me a box with a ring in it. It was a beautiful dinner ring from the '30s with diamonds and sapphires. I was touched. I was also completely oblivious as to what was about to happen. I said, "It's so beautiful, thank you."

Then David said, "Teri, will you marry me?" Whoa. I guess the ring should have been a big clue, but he may as well have offered me a tuna-fish sandwich, I was that disinterested. Was I in love with him? I didn't know. I wasn't accustomed to being attracted to anyone good or nice or decent. How could I trust that? I didn't want to say, "No, you're not the one. You're not creepy enough." I wasn't ready to give up, either. So I just said, "It's too soon." David didn't seem surprised or hurt. He accepted my answer for what it was, and we went out to dinner. I wore the ring that night, and I thought it was pretty. But it wasn't symbolic to me. I wore it off and on thereafter, but I didn't look at it as the unanswered question it represented. It was beautiful, and we were happy, and that was enough for me.

But it wasn't the same for David. Every so often, on a trip or at a romantic restaurant, he would bring it up again, saying, "How about now? Are you ready to get married now?"

A few months later I decided I wanted to move from Laurel Canyon. David thought we should buy a house together. I said, "Mmm. Maybe." But instead I bought a house on my own on Sunset Plaza Drive. When I told David, who'd been so patient and supportive, he was finally upset: "Why did you do this? What about us?" All I could say was, "I need more time on my own." I would talk to Alfa-Betty or Heidi or Jill Frank—a friend I'd met when she was an assistant director on *Firstborn*—and I'd tell them, "I don't know what to do. I don't feel like this guy knows who I really am." I felt like he was inventing an image of the person he wanted me to be, a celebrity persona that wasn't real. I figured that it was a question of time, that maybe I just hadn't known David long enough.

Somewhere in the fog of the late eighties, I flew to Mexico City to film *Miracles* with Tom Conti, Paul Rodriguez, and Christopher Lloyd. Tom Conti and I played a newly divorced couple who get abducted by thieves and taken to South America, where we have a series of adventures that reignite our romance. It took a whole lot of adventure to get that romance going again. It seemed like we were there forever—we shot in the hot sun day after day after day, all over Mexico: Mexico City, Veracruz, Acapulco.

In Mexico City we shot in a studio called Charabusco. I had a scene where I'm in a boat that sinks, and the boat was filled with cold, filthy, bug-infested water. Glamorous movie-star life—can't beat it. From there we went to Veracruz, where we were shooting in the middle of the hot desert. My character had been kidnapped on her way to a formal event, and she was wearing a long, pink, satin dress. It was unbearable in the heat, so I suggested that my character rip the bottom off her dress and make a hat out of it. The scene worked, and from then on my costume was much more desert-appropriate. Unfortunately, my next suggestion—that my character would be magically transported to an air-conditioned hotel room where she would lounge in a champagne bubble bath—didn't go over so well. David smartly waited until we were in lovely Acapulco to come visit me. He spent time on the set and made friends with everyone. He knew a little Spanish and used to say, "She is my *novia*," which meant, "She is my lover." Sweet.

The crew had a great time on the set. They'd stay out late in Mexican bars, doing tequila shots until dawn. But as the star, I had to show up for hair and makeup at 7 A.M., ready for work, so

I always holed up in the hotel and felt a bit isolated. Having David's company made the shoot much more fun for me. He'd be waiting for me when I came home from a long day, and I didn't have to go to sleep feeling like everyone was having fun except me. It's nice to have pals around when you're making movies, and it's rare that it happens.

The next summer I went to act in a play at the Williamstown Theater Festival. My early days in the Public Theater may have found me flying across the stage over a Greek chorus of penguins, but I still loved acting on the stage. There is nothing in the world like it.

At Williamstown I joined what we liked to call the Yalemafia. I was in a play called *Undiscovered Country* by Arthur Schnitzler, with Blythe Danner, Peter Riegert, Jim Naughton, and the delightful Dylan Baker. By that time, 1987, summers wasn't my best season. The heat made my body cuckoo. Again, I started in with the doctors. They attached wires to me and shocked me to see if my hand jerked properly. They gave me hearing tests and vision tests. I even had a spinal tap. Sometimes they mentioned MS as a possibility, but all the tests came back clear. They couldn't find anything. Then the symptoms would fade away and I'd forget about it, sort of. But it was starting to always hang out in the back of my mind.

During those redundant summer doctor visits, I was cast in *Full Moon in Blue Water,* a movie directed by Peter Masterson, who had just directed *The Trip to Bountiful* with Geraldine Page, one of my heroes. Gene Hackman played a widower in Texas who was trapped in the memories of his beloved wife. I played his patient girlfriend, who tries to break through his idealized memories to bring him back to the real world. This was my second time playing Gene Hackman's unfulfilled lover. Couldn't the guy make a commitment?

When you sign on to do a movie, the production company's insurance often requires that you pay a visit to one of their doctors. Needless to say, I never happened to mention my symptoms to the insurance company's doctor. I would go in, he would take my blood pressure, listen to my heart, and, presto, I was fine. I liked that about him. One time I went to the insurance doctor and he actually handed me a script to read. Was he kidding? As if I had any leverage in what got made. I smiled, took the script, and left it on top of the trash can in the lobby, figuring that if I left it on top of the trash can, a homeless person with more moviemaking influence than I had might find it and get it made. You never know in Hollywood.

So, with a clean bill of health for the insurance company, off I went to Galveston, Texas, beeping, tripping, and weak, but happy to be working. The director didn't need to know that I was sleeping twelve hours a night and could hardly feel my right leg. When I arrived, it was hot and humid. That heat! It just destroyed me. One day one of the crew guys said to me, "Why do you walk like you have a stick up your butt?" Good question. I had no idea I was walking funny. From then on, I tried consciously not to have a stick up my butt when I walked. I'd met a few people with sticks up their butts, and I sure didn't want to be one of them. So when I think of *Full Moon in Blue Water,** I remember it fondly as the stick-up-my-butt movie.

When David came down to visit me in Texas, I picked him up

*Which is never.

146

at the airport and before his luggage even bumped down the conveyor belt I was asking him about my walk. "Watch me!" I commanded, and I strode across the terminal. "You look great from every angle," he told me. But I insisted that he watch again. I wanted his honest opinion. He was a great doctor and, above all, a great diagnostician. When I told him all the symptoms and what all the doctors had said and the results of all the tests, he said simply, "I don't think it's MS." He went on to explain: "You trip and drop things, but you don't have numbness and tingling, and you don't have vision problems. You don't have any of the main symptoms of MS. If you do have a neurological disorder, I just don't think MS is something you're going to have to worry about." I know he was telling me the truth of what he knew, and that he wouldn't fudge it to protect me. I trusted his knowledge and instinct, and I still do.

Even so, the idea that my walk was noticeably off-kilter was disturbing to me. If it wasn't MS, then it had to be something else. After David went back home I called up a friend from my acting class, Alan Haufrect. Alan was from a family of Houston doctors—his father was a doctor; his brother was a doctor; I'm pretty sure even their cat knew CPR. Alan's father gave me the name of yet another doctor. He was a neurologist working out of a big medical center at the University of Houston. It was close to where we were shooting, so I made an appointment. When I entered, the nurse asked me my name and why I was there. I said "I'm Teri Garr, and I want the doctor to check me for MS." She looked at me and said, "God, I hope not! That is a nightmare!" Hello, trained professional? I should have said, "Listen, lady. You want nightmare? Try dancing on the wing of a 747 at the Academy Awards!"

This Texas doctor with the alarmist nurse turned out to be a warm, attentive listener with a hint of a Spanish accent. He put me through a bunch of diagnostic tests, which revealed that my right side was weaker than my left side. So now I had a piece of paper stating that what I knew to be true was true. Fabulous. When the Texas doctor looked at all my tests he said, "Well, maybe it is, maybe it isn't. If it *is* MS, you can go into the sun for a little bit, but not too long." Oh, that cleared everything up. The medical advice I got bore remarkable resemblance to health advice from a woman's magazine. Stay out of the sun. Drink your castor oil. Don't walk under any ladders. I was glad to get home from Texas and back to David.

The beeping, weakness, and tingling started to ebb and flow on a daily basis. It was there; it was gone. I like to say, "Whatever is going in my body, the first treatment is to ignore it." But this time denial wasn't enough. The pins and needles were there full-time. A friend of mine, comedian Jonathan Katz, always tells me, "Teri, you can't have both. Pick one: pins or needles." It was distracting and bizarre, like trying to have a picnic when you're being attacked by a swarm of gnats: You're not scared and there's no real threat, but you just can't sit still and enjoy the scenery. I had faith in the power of medicine. There had to be some kind of treatment.

So I just kept looking for answers. I went to a doctor at UCLA, and I started at the beginning. I told him all the stories of all the doctors and all the tests. He told me to relax. When a doctor says to "relax," he's saying, "You're losing it. Get a grip." And then he added his prescription to my increasing list of sophisticated scientific medical treatments. "Don't let yourself get stressed," he said. "Buy a book about meditation." Thanks, Deepak.

Weird as the doctor's advice felt at the time, I see it differently now. At the time, I thought relaxation had nothing to do with the problem. Besides, it was out of the question. I couldn't relax. I was a workaholic. I had to keep auditioning, keep working, and keep going on Letterman's and Carson's shows. Being busy felt safe. Remember, it's tough to hit a moving target. Looking back, I see that times of stress really did make my symptoms worse. I was driven, but I wasn't in the driver's seat.

I didn't buy the meditation book. If no doctor could put his finger on what was wrong with me, I sincerely doubted a ten-dollar paperback that told me to sit back, breathe deeply, and access my inner Gandhi would. I saw no choice but to keep moving forward. And my symptoms eventually receded without any diagnosis or treatment, as they always did. As soon as they went away, I put it all out of my mind almost completely. It made no sense to me to continue thinking about being sick when I felt fine. Besides, maybe whatever it was had gone away forever. I was always pretty sure that was the case.

Between meetings about parts and talk shows and social events, I was starting to have a little more down time. After *Full Moon in Blue Water*, I shot *Let It Ride* in Miami with Richard Dreyfuss. Then I did what I always did between projects—recovered, saw friends, lived life, and did laundry. Only a few years earlier there had been no gap between shooting movies, but now there were stretches of a few months during which I didn't know what would be next. This is the reality of being an actress. The jobs slow down long before you do, and you milk what's left for all it's worth. There are a million parts for twenty-year-old women, but once you hit forty, there are fewer leading comedy parts. I was up against Madeline Kahn, Sally Field, Lily Tomlin, and lots of others, and none of us was turning down much. Meanwhile, my *Tootsie* costar Dustin Hoffman had just won the Academy Award for *Rain Man*. Maybe Dustin is a special case, but men certainly have a longer Hollywood shelf life. It's a good thing he got out of that dress.

Thanks to all my talk-show appearances, I had a high TVQ—meaning TV Quotient—which meant I was considered a recognizable star and was desirable for TV movies. I was constantly shooting TV movies in Toronto and Vancouver, but they weren't *Angels in America*. Now I was playing side parts, like the crazy lawyer or the pain-in-the-neck nurse in a hostage situation—not that funny overall, but there were some amusing moments. Around 1987, director Bill Forsyth was casting the feature film *Housekeeping* for CBS. I remember hearing that everyone my age was trying out. Christine Lahti got the part. I couldn't believe there was so much worthy competition for one role. But there was always more possibility around the corner. Hoping for roles feels a lot like playing the slot machines: Two cherries line up and you think you nearly won, so you keep feeding the machine quarters.

I didn't sit around waiting for my job jackpot to roll in. I spent my down time jetting back and forth between New York and Los Angeles. I liked being bicoastal and wanted to solidify my New York base, so I passed my beloved Village rental to Griffin and bought an apartment on West Eighty-first Street. Linda Ronstadt was selling it. The real-estate agent told me that before her, Liv Ullmann and Bibi Andersson, both Ingmar Bergman leading ladies, had owned it, so I figured it had good acting karma. It was a beautiful eleventh-floor apartment across from the planetarium with a little balcony and views of the Hudson and East Rivers. Right after the closing, I went directly to the Bloomingdale's furniture department and bought some of the floor samples. They weren't the same ones I used to sit in and fantasize about, but they were close enough.

Then and there, in my apartment on West Eighty-first Street in New York City in the summer of 1988, my dream of having a home and luxuriating in a fancy Bloomingdale's living room came true at last. It was just about all it was cracked up to be.

14

Grace of My Heart

By 1988, I had known David Kipper for more than six years. We didn't live together, but he was the best boyfriend I ever had, so loving and thoughtful and supportive. But however much I tried, I couldn't make it work. I always put my work first. Whenever I got a new part, he'd be excited for me, but the first thing he'd ask was, "Where's it shooting? How long will you be gone?" He never wanted me to leave. When I think about it now, I realize he simply wanted to be with me, to hear the details of my day, to share small moments, to wake up with me in the morning. That's what love is supposed to be, right? But at the time it felt possessive and suffocating. The relationship just wasn't my priority. Watching my mother toil to keep our family together had put the fear in me. It taught me to be self-sufficient, to take of myself and never depend on a man, or, as my friend Billy Al once said to me, "Be a self-feeder." But was I too independent to make room for anyone else? I still dreamed about settling down and starting a family. I wanted a noisy house with a bunch of kids and home-cooked meals. But when it came to the reality of intimacy, I balked (at least in this case I did). I was afraid that David's love came with a price—my career or my independence—and whatever it was, I didn't want to pay it. Sometimes the things you don't say define your relationship.

Our breakup took years. It was horrible, prolonged, and crazy. I'd tell my friends, "I don't know how to break up with him; it really isn't working." Then I'd tell David he was perfect, but I wasn't ready. He'd be gracious; we'd try to be friends; we'd have dinner; and we'd end up getting back together. This happened so many times I'm ashamed to count them. I never got over the sense that he was in love with the movie-star version of me, that he didn't see who I really was. As that notion grew, it killed the chemistry for me. I really trusted him, though, and it would prove hard to find anyone I trusted as much ever again. He set the bar high—maybe too high.

Later that year I went to Cannes to promote *Full Moon in Blue Water*. It had been a long time since my trip to the south of France for *The Conversation*. Back then I'd been an unknown actress tagging along with the Coppola contingent. Now I was a member of the Academy, but I was alone. The beach was a sea of paparazzi, taking photos of starlets coming out of the water wearing seaweed. I had traveled straight from Texas to France, and in between my relationship had fallen apart. The glamour of Cannes was wasted on me. What I needed was time to decompress.

For all my issues, I really loved David, and his sudden absence left me floating. What had gone wrong? I was in my extremely late thirties. Why was I still alone? Anyone with any sense could see that David would make a perfect husband. If I couldn't make it work with him, would I ever have the family I wanted? With these questions unresolved, I did what anyone who's adrift should do: I went directly to Paris.

A trip to Paris; what better way to put my life in perspective? If there is such a thing as past lives, then I must have lived a few of mine in Paris. The steel gray sky and the perpetually wet streets create a dramatic mood. I'd walk along those streets remembering the stories my aunt Grace had told me about being in the Folies Bergère in the '30s. How being in the same city as Hemingway, Picasso, Henry Miller, and Sartre had transformed her life forever. Now, decades later, I was an actress in Paris, strolling down the Rive Gauche, trying to be existential. I wasn't sure where it would take me, but that was okay. I felt strong when I was there, and I needed to feel strong after breaking up with David.

When I was a kid we always had some "aunt" or "uncle" staying at our house—at least I thought they were aunts and uncles. Years later I would find out that they were just a dance team from Cleveland or a dog act from Philly, all part of our extended gypsy family. As my parents' vaudeville friends made their way to California in search of fame and fortune, they would crash with us until they got settled, got their big breaks, or left town in defeat. Not many left town as proof of the old vaudeville spirit. They would rather slowly fade into obscurity than admit defeat.

My favorite of these uncles and aunts were Nikko and Grace. Nikko was an intense, nomadic Russian. In the 1920s he escaped the Russian Revolution and fled to Paris to be in the Folies Bergère. That's where he met my aunt Grace, who also escaped— from Atlantic City—to dance in the Folies. They had a comedy dance act, whatever that is. They would do some ballet lift, and Grace's finger would end up in Nikko's nose. (They did this for a *living,* okay?) They got married and decided they should be movie stars, so they moved to Los Angeles, with lots of joie de vivre and no money. Grace had been in the Rockettes with my mother, so she and Nikko came for a night and stayed for a while—quite a while. They lived with us off and on for what seemed like years. The only thing they ever did in Hollywood was a dance scene in *Abbott and Costello Meet the Mummy.* We used to watch it and shout, "Yahoo! That's Grace and Nikko." It never occurred to us that while Abbott and Costello were known for many achievements, their fabulous dance numbers were not among them.

Grace and Nikko had vamped a million moneymaking schemes to hold them over until the show-business work picked up, which they thought should be any minute now. At one point they had an Orange Julius stand in the Farmers' Market, a collection of wooden stalls where people sell everything from pottery to tacos. The Farmers' Market is an L.A. institution, and I loved having friends there. During that time Nikko was a maître d' at the Villa Capri, a very popular restaurant in Hollywood. The owner, Patsy D'Amour, also had a pizza stand in the Farmers' Market. Patsy and his brother Franklin were ex-performers. On the side they were all great cooks so naturally they opened restaurants, and good ones. (Patsy's Pizza in the Farmers' Market is still the best pizza in town.) These people made up the rather awkward foundation of my extended family. From them I would hear about places in Europe where they ate goat's head for dinner and thought it was a delicacy. (In contrast to this, my Brownie meetings at North Hollywood Park seemed . . . well . . . dull.) Through them, I was exposed to another slice of the world, while smelling the orange blossoms in my little Valley backyard. I was determined to check out this other world someday if I could.

Patsy's restaurant was frequented by James Dean and Frank Sinatra, among other celebrity types. This was one of Nikko's better jobs, and it allowed him and Grace to move into their own house, a very interesting log cabin in Sherman Oaks. I loved staying there with Grace and Nikko. It was a dark little house with no bedrooms, only balconies. Its one room had wooden rafters and a white bear rug on the floor, complete with snarling teeth. But that didn't last long. One day James Dean came to the restaurant looking for a place to live. Nikko immediately rented their tiny house to him, and he and Grace moved back in with us.

I know I'm probably the only one in the world, but I had a major crush on James Dean. Grace and Nikko were sympathetic to my situation, so they let my brother and me mow their famous tenant's lawn. My brother did most of the mowing, while I did all of the lusting. When Dean died, we helped Grace clean out the house. His essence was everywhere. He had hung a noose over the rafters. There was an unfinished clay sculpture he had been working on, as well as photos, bongo drums, and tons of books everywhere. My brother and I came across an eight-millimeter movie he had made when he was filming *Giant* with Elizabeth Taylor and Dennis Hopper. At one point the camera lingered on Elizabeth getting up from a chair. I guess I'm not the only one who was starstruck.

At any rate, let it be stated for the record that, years later, Dennis Hopper borrowed the film and never gave it back. I'm still waiting . . .

When my mother went off to work, Grace would play with me. We'd draw, talk, and design inventions like goggles that kept the fumes away from your eyes when you were chopping onions. Those goggles were going to make us rich! When my mother was around it was a free-for-all, but Grace had rules. She taught me boundaries. She'd say, "You can't color on my paper. You have to color on your own paper," or "You can use a little of this lotion, but you can't touch my toothbrush or my hairbrush." Grace was nurturing, but she gave me structure. My mother provided for us, but Grace filled in some of the blanks for me.

Grace is the person who sold me on show business. My parents were too busy and disillusioned to sell me on their unfulfilled dreams, but Grace's showbiz world was different. For hours I lay on the floor at her feet, engrossed in stories about Paris. She told me about Josephine Baker, Mistinguett, and the feathered costumes she wore in her life as a dancer. It all sounded so exciting. I had to be a dancer like Grace and my mom. It was Grace's stories that made me beg my mother for dance lessons. I loved her, and I loved the direction she'd given me. She tried to make me see that as show people we were "different"; we were more resilient, we were generous, and we watched out for each other. She also taught me that it was okay to live life on the fly.

Grace died of a heart attack when I was nineteen. She had a rheumatic heart. It was only when she died that I realized she was always around our house because she was ill, that we were supposed to be taking care of her. I was devastated when she died, and Nikko was ruined. He worshipped her, and so did I, in my own way.

Grace taught me the expression "You always meet someone you know on the Champs-Elysées." On this post-Cannes trip, I sat having a glass of wine at a café on the Champs and bumped into the Hollywood superagent Swifty Lazar. Swifty was always very nice to me. He often invited me to his Academy Awards party at Spago, *the* party to go to, a small gathering of celebrities and moguls from Sophia Loren, Cary Grant, and Jack Lemmon to Andy Warhol, Oprah Winfrey, and Rupert Murdoch. When Swifty saw me he said, "What the hell are you doing here, Miss Garr? Can I buy you a drink?" He sat and told me stories of being in Paris with Bogey and Bacall (or "Betty," as he called her), wild stories about drinking and hanging out at the Folies Bergères. Oh, that Bogey.

I told him about Nikko and Grace and how they had gone from the Folies to the Farmers' Market. He loved the story. I imagined his life in Paris with Bacall, staying on the rich side of the city at the Georges V with the Bogarts—much different than my take on the place, but just as provocative. Swifty and I had met dozens of times before, usually at parties, and here we were in Paris, making small talk on the Champs-Elysées. (Swifty also said that I should write a book about my life, and that he would be my agent. I'm never going to write a book, thought I. But in the immortal words of David Mamet, "Things change.")

From the beautiful city of lights to the oil-slicked, sulfur-reeking harbor of San Pedro, life was good. I spent the rest of that summer in San Pedro shooting the extremely forgettable movie *Out Cold* with John Lithgow and Randy Quaid. But my mind was elsewhere. It wasn't until Thanksgiving that I felt like myself again. I often hosted Thanksgiving with my relatives—my mother, my brother Ed and his family, my brother Phil, my aunts Alice and Terry, and lots of friends. My mother and I would cook for days. That year Toni Basil brought her boyfriend Spazz Attack, a dancer from a Devo video with an orange mohawk. Marshall and Alfa-Betty came, as they usually did. And my aunt Alice, who wore Coke-bottle glasses and always told dirty jokes after she'd had a few Manhattans. The evening ended with my sister-in-law's mother smoking a pack of Kents and telling stories about how her musician husband used to play bass with Benny Goodman's saxophonist Toots Mondello.

This was my family, a hodgepodge of blood relatives and friends, and they made my life feel complete. I could spend my time trying to figure out what was wrong with my body, or I could eat turkey, listen to Toni Basil's never-ending stories of dance class, zone out on tryptophan, and appreciate what I had.

15

With Friends Like These . . .

For me, sex was always about being intimate with someone emotionally, but for years I put my career first and starting a family second. After coming so close with David Kipper, I started thinking I might finally be ready to start having kids. But now, as I wrapped up another inconsequential wife role in *Short Time,* an action movie starring Dabney Coleman, it dawned on me that I wasn't getting any younger. Ticktock.

I had always, always wanted a baby. My reasons weren't complicated: I just wanted to buy baby carriages and little frilly bassinets. No, I instinctively wanted to nurture. And change diapers. I imagined I'd be pretty good at this, based on nothing. While I devoted everything to my career, part of me thought of showbiz life as just a phase. Filler, actually, until my real calling as "earth mother" revealed itself. At some point I'd get married, have kids, and have a real life, like Ozzie and Harriet, right? (It doesn't get any realer than that.)

One August night in 1989, I drove home from a guest appearance on *The Tonight Show* and pulled into the driveway of my dark house. I was starving, and I opened the refrigerator to scrounge around for a snack. The contents of the refrigerator were colorless—takeout containers and dinner leftovers in their nondescript white boxes. I thought, I was just on national television. I could run for president! And here I am, alone in an empty, cold, dark house, eating stale nuts. This isn't a life. The life that I'd wanted so much wasn't complete without someone to come home to.

Gloria Steinem once said, "I have yet to hear a man ask for advice on how to combine marriage and a career." I always liked that quotation. I suppose I considered myself a feminist. I wanted to be conventional but saw the whole thing as a dead-end street. Yet maybe there was a way for a man and a woman to be together without the woman being subservient, or something like that. (I was really not into the details.) All I ever saw in Hollywood were what seemed like these strange business arrangements people called marriages, and a lot of divorces when the mergers fell out of favor. In L.A., being married didn't mean much; the only time you got any respect was if the movie you were in racked up big grosses. Oh, I admit my whole perception was pretty skewed, but something was missing . . . and not just from the refrigerator.

A few months earlier, at the end of 1988, I'd met a man who I thought was a contender for the role of husband. I was at a premiere for a movie called *Punchline,* starring Sally Field and Tom Hanks. The party was in the parking lot next to Grauman's Chinese Theater. It was a big studio party—one of those parties that feels like a wedding, under a big white tent with lots of candles, extravagant flower arrangements, multiple food stations, and gift bags heavy with perfume samples and other designer goodies. A handsome, dark-haired man in a perfectly tailored suit came up to me and introduced himself as Lloyd (not his real name; from now on I'll just refer to him as S*#T). He told me we had friends in common.

The next day, a friend called and told me that her friend had met me and wanted to take me out. What friend? I wondered. I didn't remember him. Later, when I met him officially, I liked him. There were some warning signs—he was in show business, he was unemployed, he was kind of slick, he drove a Jaguar, and he looked exactly like my father. But nobody's perfect. As I was driving home I couldn't stop thinking about him and how attractive he was. When he asked me out again, I was thrilled. I didn't have the greatest track record for picking men, but I was head over heels for this guy. He understood my world, he was dapper, charming, and funny, and I fell for him.

Because David Kipper had been such a prince of a man, I had somehow dropped my guard and begun thinking that all men were that thoughtful, honest, and true. Can you imagine? Instead of taking the time to get to know S*#T, I projected those qualities onto him and decided that we were a perfect match. Sure, he often left my house at two in the morning, even when I said, "Please, please stay." David never would have done that, but in this case I didn't see it as a lack of commitment; instead, I saw it as quirkiness. I thought he was like me—career oriented and always on the go. Sure, he was living with another woman when we met, but he told me it was over. I took it all at face value and helped him find a house.

Still, I was auditioning him for a bigger role, so the Friday after my *Tonight Show* late-night revelation, I sat S*#T down at my kitchen table and said, "I really want to have a baby." I reminded him that I was 39.999 years old and there was no time to waste. I said that if he didn't want to go along with my plan, I understood. It was no problem. I would find someone who would. I just didn't want to pussyfoot around. But S*#T was completely unfazed. He said, "Okay, great." That was the answer I wanted, and I wanted it so badly that I didn't pay attention to the nature of our conversation. I didn't notice that it was devoid of romance. I was oblivious to the transactional tone of our resolution. Come to think of it, I'm the one who set that tone in the first place. In an ideal world, there's a little more passion when babies are conceived, but I was too determined to worry about the emotional groundwork— or the real world, for that matter.

Maybe as a consequence of that, getting pregnant wasn't the frolicking afternoon delight I'd imagined. I'd take my temperature, call S*#T, and say, "My temperature is elevated. It's time! Come right over." He'd agreeably appear. This went on for a couple of months, but I was impatient so I decided to go to a fertility clinic to speed things up. I started giving myself hormone injections. It wasn't the sexiest process, but I assumed that the end would more than justify the means.

I didn't plan to give up my career, and I knew it would be hard to balance being an actor and a mother. But combining career and motherhood is hard for most women, including my own mother, so why not me? She'd given me and my brothers a loving, fun-packed childhood while she struggled to make ends meet. I wasn't struggling; in fact, I decided all I needed was a little extra cash, and I could do anything. And as much as I admired my mother's ability to make something from nothing, I looked forward to giving my daughter (or son) a real dollhouse instead of one made of rocks.

I started getting ready for the challenge of balancing my career with my future family. I busied myself reading books about child-rearing and caught myself eyeing overpriced onesies in store windows on Rodeo Drive. My baby fantasies snowballed out of control with the temptation of all this precious baby stuff. But I was preparing myself for the wrong challenges. A double whammy of betrayals awaited me—the first wreaking havoc with my career, the second destroying my dream of a perfect family.

The first betrayal came from two of my closest friends. My parents had taught me the value of friendship. They treated their friends—my "aunts" and "uncles"—like family, and I looked at my friends the same way. We looked out for each other. If my friend Toni was sick, I'd bring her homemade soup. If I was on the road and needed to talk, I knew Alfa-Betty and Marshall, my old friends from the Actors Studio, were always there for me. Toni, Heidi, Jill, Arlene, Griffin—I prided myself on having great friends. But over the years, especially when I was traveling in the fast lane, my "friendar" was erratic, and some of my choices were way off. This is a side effect of going from obscurity to fame: You don't know who to trust, and you're too busy to figure it out. Besides, I wasn't programmed not to trust.

As much as I failed to choose the right men, I didn't spend enough time evaluating the reliability of my friends. So, as always, naïveté (not to be confused with stupidity) was my operative instinct. I gave everyone the benefit of the doubt and kept going forward without paying attention to anything but my career.

I had talked to my closest friends and family about my physical symptoms—of course David knew, as did Heidi, Toni, and Alfa-Betty. They were discreet people, and I trusted them. I spent half my time feeling perfectly healthy and conveniently forgetting there was anything wrong with me, and the other half I spent being fed up with my ongoing symptoms. It was a never-ending battle between being in denial and wanting answers. Whenever the answer-seeking side dominated, I sought out a new doctor in hope of gleaning new information or insight.

In 1989 I still hadn't been officially diagnosed, and I heard about a doctor in Boston who was a specialist in MS. He was supposed to be the very best. When I set up the appointment, I mentioned it to a friend. Let's call her Clytemnestra just for fun. Now, I thought Cly was to be trusted, but she was a common breed in Hollywood; a person with no self-respect who only felt alive when in the company of fame. It's a pretty common Hollywood affliction, but difficult to spot sometimes. This type of person gains power through flattery, charm, and plain old butt-kissing. We were good friends at the time. What can I say? Flattery works. Ask Michael Eisner.

So Clytemnestra talked to another friend, let's call her Medea. Cly and Med got together and decided that the possibility of Teri Garr having a serious chronic illness was the juiciest gossip they had ever heard. And gossip is currency, especially in Hollywood, so why wait for a diagnosis from a card-carrying physician when they could diagnose me instead?

I think they said it like, "Puh-leeze, don't tell anybody because she doesn't want anyone to know, but TERI GARR HAS MS. IT'S TRUE!!" Which only made people want to repeat the rumor. Agh. Human nature. They told *everyone* I had MS. And I mean everyone. They may as well have set up a "Teri Garr has MS phone tree," using the 90210 phone book as a starting point.

Apparently, my "friends" were right: It *was* juicy gossip. Soon the entire world knew for certain that I had MS, even before I did.

I woke up one morning, ran a couple of miles at the gym, came home, drank a glass of orange juice, and suddenly I was in Condolence Central. The phone started ringing. Friends, former colleagues, acquaintances—everyone was calling to ask if I really had MS and whether I was okay. Even people I'd seen only days or months before at dinners or at parties seemed to think I'd become permanently confined to a wheelchair overnight. Maybe I should have been moved by the groundswell of sympathy. But it caught me off-guard, and I had trouble accepting the misguidedness of it. I tried to be patient. I would say, "No, not according to my doctor. Thanks for asking." It was like picking up a tabloid and finding out I had had Muhammad Ali's illegitimate child.

Hollywood has its own culture, so the inquiries about my health ranged from caring to catty. But that wasn't the real problem; the gossip had an immediate and devastating effect on my career. I was still reading scripts, and I still felt like I was in the game. But what might have been a lull or the beginning of a slow drop-off became much worse as soon as word hit the street that I had MS. My work opportunities fell off a cliff. It was a done deal. The phone was ringing with inquiries about my health, but when it came to inquiries about my availability for roles, it was adios amigos. The press was hungry to know more, but the industry was sated. I wasn't special. This is the standard way the industry reacts to actor illnesses. David Lander, who played Squiggy on *Laverne and Shirley,* was sitting in the lobby of Warner Bros. once, waiting to audition, when he heard the receptionist take a call. She told the person at the other end of the line that the part was no longer available. But after she hung up she said, "That was Richard Pryor's agent, trying to get him up for this part. Can you imagine? He has MS!" David, who also has MS but was up for the same part, was speechless. I know what he was thinking: Title I and Title V of the Americans with Disabilities Act prohibit employment discrimination against qualified individuals with disabilities. Or maybe he was thinking, I hope I have time to get a hamburger after this. What do I know? I'm not a psychic, even though I played one on *ER*.

When the offers stopped coming in, my agents didn't mention discrimination. My "actress mind" went right to thinking, I stink. They gave me the party line: "Things are slow right now. They're slow all over. There's nothing much out there for actresses your age." Age is a reality every Hollywood actress knows she's going to have to face at some point. But my age hadn't been an issue until the MS rumors started. Plus, I never thought I was an actress who worked because of my looks. I was real. But whatever this "MS" was, the industry wanted no part of it—and my agents were no exception. This is CAA, a talent agency fondly known in Hollywood as "The Evil Empire." Let's just say they don't specialize in warm and cuddly, which is fine when you're a healthy young actress, your career is on the rise, and you need a team of people to fend off the scripts being thrown your way. But after the "news" of my illness hit the papers, the reaction from that place was chilly, to say the least. I practically had to spell my name to get anyone to take my calls.

At first I was outraged. Whatever was going on with my body had been going on for years. It never got in the way of my work. Diagnosis or no diagnosis, I knew it was unfair for the jobs to stop coming. It was as if I'd been fired on the basis of a rumor! If I'd had an office job, I could have sued. But actors are freelancers, and it was the easiest thing in the world for directors to decide I wasn't "right" for a part. I had no recourse.

Now, don't forget, as an actress I have a fragile ego. The insecurity I'd learned to work through over the years surged back to the surface. I watched movies like *Beetlejuice* and *All of Me* come out and knew that my name hadn't even come up for consideration. I was off the radar. I lost confidence. I started thinking that the job offers had disappeared because I'd been pulling the wool over everyone's eyes. Now they realized that I stunk as an actress and had no talent. Ha—I knew it was only a matter of time, the jig was up. It was a tough trio: a series of mysterious symptoms that I still didn't understand, my insecurities about my acting ability, and the reality of being an "aging" actress. Add to that the size of my breasts (small) and the size of my ego (large), and my hopelessness shot off the charts. I was an emotional train wreck.

It wasn't like I was blacklisted—I still got jobs—but it sure felt like I wasn't getting my share of the really good stuff. The question for me was, Why? With the benefit of age, experience, and hindsight, however, I'm confident that the gossip was the primary reason my work slowed down. My body was not in bad shape. There were no outwardly visible symptoms, now that I'd stopped walking as if I had a stick up my butt. My acting abilities certainly hadn't disappeared. Hollywood had leapt to the judgment that MS was completely incapacitating and my career took a nosedive, taking with it my self-confidence. When I did have meetings with my agents, I acted crazy, paranoid, and defensive. Who wouldn't want that? In short—and I can finally say this without reservation—these rumors caused me big trouble. In my estimation, I missed a good ten years of work because of some "harmless" gossip.

I didn't talk to my mother about what was going on. She was seventy-nine years old and was starting to show signs of dementia. She kept calling the police to report that all her jewelry had been stolen when the truth was she couldn't remember where she kept it. I moved her into an assisted-living facility. She couldn't stand it and kept leaving on whichever bus came to the stop first. She thought the residence was a waste of money—I'd lie to her and say it was covered by her pension, saying, "You know how you got this? From the government. You earned this from being a Rockette. It's all yours." We tried a few different places, but she was never happy. Then her younger sister, my aunt Terry, started having troubles of her own in Sarasota, Florida. She was spending all her money on lottery tickets and was overwhelmed with solicitations from religious organizations and, I think, God himself. But Aunt Terry refused to move. So Alfa-Betty and I flew down to Florida and kidnapped her. We told her we were taking her for a drive, and we were—straight to the airport. She was pretty out of it, but on the plane we told her she was going to see my mother, Phyllis, and she said, "Oh, good." We arrived at my mother's assisted-living home at eleven at night. Aunt Terry knocked on my mother's door and said, "Hey, kiddo." They were so cute. Alfa-Betty and I smiled at each other. From then on, my mother and aunt lived together and kept each other as grounded as possible.

So I didn't talk to my mother about my career woes—or my health woes, for that matter. I only told her the good things, and even if I'd told her the bad things, she wouldn't have heard them. Instead, I turned to my oldest friends for support. It wasn't really my style to weep on their shoulders, but they took me out to dinner, kept me busy, and went shopping with me for clothes, to remind me that I still had a body to hang them on.

For me to rise above the rumors and to be confident about my career was really, really hard. Thanks to Clytemnestra and Medea for helping; what are friends for, right? My showbiz mom always taught me to hold my cards close to my chest. She knew that in show business it's not who you are inside that counts, it's your public persona that keeps you working. That was the age of zero introspection. We kind of worked from the outside out. We hid secrets about my father and his problems; she instructed me to keep the bad things the boys did to me in the woodshed to myself. I was reared to plaster up a perfect facade, no matter how slipshod it was, and to live in that contraption.

16

Walking on Broken Glass

My "friendar" was spotty enough, but my "love-relationshipdar" had gone utterly haywire. I started to believe that getting pregnant and starting a family with S*#T might sustain me as my career fell off a cliff. I knew that when a baby came along, my priorities would shift. But S*#T wasn't exactly supportive when the rumors hit the fan. He was as blasé and dismissive as my agents were. It didn't occur to me at the time that this was a bad sign. I guess I was still used to fending for myself. But then I started to notice that my boyfriend was busier than usual. He had a lot of "business meetings." I suppose I should have begun to wonder when many of these "meetings" ran so late that he wouldn't even come to my house for the night. You'd think a girl would pick up on something like that.

But I trusted him. I mean, he wasn't just any old boyfriend. We were planning to have a baby together. Why would he say he wanted to have a family if he didn't mean it? Why else would we be doing all this fertility crap? It sure *seemed* like we were on the same page—especially when he was looking to co-produce a TV pilot that Warner Bros. was pitching me to do. At the same time, I was confusing my need for a sperm donor with love. Why didn't I see the writing on the wall? Because I was all hopped up on hormones and had baby on the brain. I was blindly determined to have a family with the man I thought I loved. (And I drop the word *thought* like an anvil.)

Then, on November 14, 1989, at 4:12 A.M., the phone rang. I fumbled to answer it, disoriented. Had something gone wrong? Was my mother okay? An unfamiliar voice asked, "Is this Teri Garr?" I said, "Yes," and the voice informed me that she had been sleeping with my so-called boyfriend since August, that she had caught him in bed with (yet) another woman that morning, and that she had thrown all his potted plants into his pool. I looked at the phone and tapped it on the nightstand a few times. Hmm, I thought. She went on to tell me many other things, including that he told her we were just business partners. He would drive her around in my Mercedes and tell her it was his car. Wasn't his Jaguar impressive enough? I wondered. I guess he wanted her to think he had a fleet. This woman, who was an aspiring actress by the way, had looked in the glove compartment and found my registration, the little Nancy Drew. The conversation droned on with ever more amazing details. I finally hung up, wishing this lovely woman good luck in her career.

I let all this pertinent information stew for a while. It simmered and percolated in my head while I sat frozen on my bed. I was so full of rage, I couldn't even move. Of course, I felt hurt and betrayed, but also stunned. After a few minutes I stood up. It was only five in the morning. It wasn't even light out yet, but there was no way I could go back to sleep. I started recalling all the lies he must have told me—times he was "stuck at the car wash" or "the traffic was bad" and he couldn't meet me. I still wasn't over-the-top upset, but I decided, quite rationally, I thought, to return some of the items he'd left at my home: socks, underwear, shirts, some old baby pictures, some debris that was left in my closet. He was moving on; surely he'd want his things immediately. While I was throwing stuff in a box, I noticed a hammer and thought I'd put that in there, too, for no particular reason.

By the time I finished, it was 7 A.M. I dumped everything in my car and drove to his house. Now I understand how murders are committed. As I sped along, nothing could have stopped me. If someone had knocked on the window and said, "Here's a million dollars in cash—just stop the car," I would have said, "I'm sorry, you'll have to keep your money. I'm on a mission here." The theme from *Rocky* was playing in my head.

I pulled up to his rented home. It was a small, yellow, ranch-style tract house in the cheaper section of Bel Air. I got out of the car with the cardboard box full of crap and headed up to the front door. I stood on the porch and rang the doorbell about eighty-seven times. No answer. Since he didn't come to the door, I assumed that he was with the other other woman. Okay, fine. I started hurling his stuff against the front of the house, yelling, "Here's your socks and your clean underwear I just washed." I emptied the box. And when I got to the bottom I thought, Oh, what's this? It's a hammer. I picked it up and, with all my strength, started smashing all the windows, one window after another. The living-room windows, the dining-room windows, the little square garage-door windows. CRASH, CRASH, CRASH. I had never smashed a window before, but as it turned out, I was pretty good at it. Once I started, I couldn't stop. When I finally got around to the kitchen windows, there he was—on the phone. I figured he was calling the police and that it was a good time for me to wrap things up. I started swearing at him in my best Irish-Catholic Valley-girl vocabulary. He just stared at me. I always wondered what he was thinking at that moment.

After I felt that was enough, I staggered back to my car. There, in the bushes, was a security guard pointing a gun at me. When he saw me, he recognized me and lowered his weapon. Ah, the power of celebrity. Getting a better table at a restaurant is one thing, but I was very pleased to have a fan in the Bel Air security patrol. The policeman said, "Oh, Ms. Garr! Are you all right?" This polite fellow assumed I was the victim. Well, in a sense I *was*, right? I answered, "I am now." I drove away feeling strangely satisfied. As soon as it was a decent hour, I called Alfa-Betty, Toni, and my other friends and told them what I'd done. Some tried to calm me down, some said "I told you so," and one said, "I'm weeding the lawn, can you call me back?"

Later that day, I went to an opening at an art gallery. If nothing else, I wasn't going to let this whole sordid thing ruin my sense of art. In the art show there was a painting of a cow in a mud puddle up to its knees. It looked to me like it should be called *In Deep Sh*t*. I decided to buy it as a little reminder of this . . . break-through (pardon the pun).

There were lots of people at the opening, and, believe me, I told my story to anyone who would listen. Someone would say, "How are you?" and I'd say, "I'll tell you how I am. Listen to this: Blah, blah, blah." The more people I told, the more it seemed like a common scenario. It seems this sort of thing happens quite a bit, and not just in L.A., though this city seems to attract more slime than usual. The reactions to betrayal are varied and fascinating. One girl found her vain boyfriend cheating, so she snuck into his house and cut off the left leg of each of his Gucci and Armani suits. Another simply put a garden hose in the bathroom window when she knew he was out of town and let the water run for a few days—nice and simple. One of my favorites was the woman who took the dog and shaved her name into the fur on its back. That way the new girlfriend would have to ask, "Who's Judy?" until the dog's hair grew back. Sometimes less is more.

A few days after the incident I had lunch with my agents at CAA. I told them the story of the windows. When I finished, there was an uncomfortable silence, as if they were thinking, "We mess around on *our* wives, and no one breaks our windows. She doesn't sound well. Maybe we should pull back. Anyway, her breasts aren't that big." Okay, maybe they didn't think all that, but I could see them squinting their eyes and looking at me sideways. So if rumors of MS hadn't completely put the kibosh on my career, I sealed the deal over lunch with my agents. I'm sure they thought I'd lost it.

When I finally stopped telling the world about my *kristallnacht,* at least a year later, I had nothing to talk about anymore. I was spent. I'd thought I would be with this guy forever, and the betrayal rankled every level of my being. His treachery hurt more than the arduous twenty-year process of trying to figure out what was wrong with my body. MS might make life a little more challenging, but betrayal just plain sucks.

That year was a hard year, and the years that followed were also tough. My personal life was in tatters. I doubted my friendships. I'd been betrayed by the man I thought I'd wanted to be with forever. My dream of having a baby was indefinitely post-poned, my career was failing, and there was something going on with my leg. I had worked my way up in show business, done okay, and peaked, and now it seemed I was in limbo. I wasn't sure I had the right perspective on that. I thought I was having a rough day, a rough week, a rough month. I figured things had to change soon. But anytime I let my mind rest I arrived at the disappoint-ing feeling of being betrayed. But I went on with my life, anyway, as best as I could, and focused on my health.

I finally took a train from New York to Boston for the doctor's appointment I had been putting off. My old friend Jill came with me. We arrived at Brigham and Women's Hospital, and they pre-pared me for my first MRI. I told Jill, "This won't take long." To-day when a patient has an MRI, she lies down and is slid under a large white magnet while classical music plays. But the MRIs of the '80s were narrow metal tubes that were extremely claustro-phobic. As soon as they put me in I freaked out and banged on the walls of the tube, screaming, "Let me out! Let me out!" They brought me out and said, "What's wrong? Are you claustropho-bic?" I said, "No, I'm fine," but ten minutes later I was yelling again. Four hours later I returned to the waiting room, and there was Jill. She looked different—bigger, stronger, more powerful. I said, "Guess it took longer than I thought. They did two MRIs, one with dye and one without." She answered, "What do you think of my new look?" She had been waiting for so long that she had fashioned shoulder pads for herself out of the paper towels in the bathroom. I had to admit they were flattering. They gave her that stylish quarterback look reminiscent of my Academy Awards splendor. I love people who use their time constructively.

I always felt like it was an imposition to ask friends to go to doctors' appointments with me, but it sure was nice to see a friendly face in the waiting room afterward. It's important to have company during all the poking and prodding of your body. (No, I'm not talking about group sex.) But sometimes the doctor's visits wore me down. The frustration of not knowing what was going on, the mercurial symptoms, and the doctors' skepticism were grueling at times. Jill was great to have around because she was patient, and creative, and she wasn't taking notes for the press, just designing clothes.

Eventually, after all the rumors and the toll on my career, I received word from the Boston doctor. He said, "Something's going on with you—I don't know what it is, but it's not MS." Talk about anticlimactic. He was the head doctor there, and he continues to be one of the leading MS neurologists in the world. Yet he went on to say, "Well, let's keep in touch. Let me know if anything changes. If I figure something out, I'll let you know."

I was relieved that I didn't have MS, but I was still plagued by my unexplained symptoms. What I didn't know then was that MS is very sneaky. I like to say MS is to disease what Enron is to accounting. No rules. It's a big fat cheater.

17

Ms. Garr Goes to Washington

I had a feeling that work would be my refuge. At first, when I was asked to do a series of Fruit of the Loom ads, I turned down the offer. "Underwear ads? No way. I'm an actress." But the pay was great, and I wasn't exactly overwhelmed with work. Besides, final photo approval was part of the deal. It crossed my mind that people I respected, like Meryl Streep or Anne Bancroft, wouldn't model underpants, but I felt that they were in a better position than I to hold out for great jobs. So I just crossed my fingers and convinced myself that no one would see the ads, anyway.

The print ad showed me in pink, yellow, and blue pastel underpants, with a tasteful jersey on top. When we were doing the shoot, they kept telling me to smile. I kept saying, "Wouldn't a subtle Mona Lisa smile be appropriate? As if she were standing in front of Leonardo in her underpants?" They just stared blankly at me. They wanted a big, happy grin.

When the ads came out, they were all over the place. It seemed like everywhere I went someone said, "I saw you in those under-pants." When I met the country singer Clint Black at an annual benefit for Ford's Theatre in Washington, D.C., he told me that he had the ad pinned up in his tour bus. Yikes. I chose to take that as a compliment. Although it seemed to me that the ads were more popular with men than women, apparently Fruit of the Loom sales skyrocketed. The commercials and ads were deemed a big success, so the next year they wanted me back.

At the time I was considering signing with my current man-agers, Brillstein/Grey. They told me, "If you sign with us, we'll double your deal." And they did, so I signed. Yes, greed had set in. Slightly. I figured, If I'm going to sell my ass, I might as well sell it big. (Not my big ass.) I must say of all the talent companies in this town, they have been the most loyal to me. They are a classy outfit.

For the second round of ads Fruit of the Loom hired a hot young commercial director. He was funny and creative. He mocked up an ad with me wearing the cute (and comfortable!) 100 percent cotton underpants and a leather jacket, perched on a mo-torcycle. I was saying, "My mother always told me to wear clean underwear in case I got in an accident." It was true. My mother always did tell me that. But that wasn't the idea that Fruit of the Loom wanted people to have about their underwear. Doughy adult men dressed up as grapes and apples? Good. Celebrity ac-tress straddling a motorcycle? Bad. Every ad the director thought up, they rejected, so eventually he was fired. I must have been considered an accomplice of sorts because I got fired, too. They paid me off, though, so no harm done. I wasn't exactly dying to appear in those ads. But I learned this lesson: Underpants are not funny (well, maybe if you wear them on your head), so don't try to tell anyone at Fruit of the Loom that they are.

Through the years, people had always told me I should have my own television series. Not one like *The Sonny and Cher Comedy Hour,* where I was a sidekick, but one in which I was the star. I was never really that interested in playing the same character over and over again. As long as my movie career was going well, I didn't think much about TV. At the time, it was definitely considered a step down. But once I'd hit the tender age of forty, the television offers were starting to look pretty good. Also, I always thought that if the project was well written, what's the difference?

I turned down plenty of television offers, until I was handed a script for a sitcom called *Good and Evil.* It was a Witt/Thomas/ Harris Productions venture. Witt/Thomas/Harris were the much respected producers of *Soap, Benson,* and *The Golden Girls.* Starring in a show of their creation seemed like a smart thing to do, and it was a pretty funny script. *Good and Evil* was about two sisters. They wanted me to play the good sister. But the night when "If I Had a Hammer" had become "I Do Have a Hammer!" was a fresh and painful memory. I'd just been double-crossed, and I was in no mood to play the good girl. I said, "I'll do it if I can be the evil one. I think I've been the nice one for too long." The evil sister spent money like water, had tons of diamonds, and cheated on all her boyfriends. She sounded great to me. Margaret Whitton, who'd just played the "rich bitch" in *Major League,* was cast as the good sister who was—what else?—working in a lab, trying to cure cancer. The brilliant Tony-winning actress Marion Seldes played our hoity-toity mother.

The show was supposed to mock the shallowness of the rich. Pretty deep subject, that shallowness. The atmosphere on the set of that "comedy" was deadly serious, and I think the producers were only half committed to the idea, since they were pretty damn rich and weren't really going to mock themselves. My appreciation for Lucille Ball quadrupled as a result of that experience.

I grew up listening to my mom say, "The director wants the woman to look like a German spy, but she's poor and it has to feel like this is the first new dress she's had in a long time. The director wants this feeling from the character." My mother always made the costumes to fit the desires of the director. That's what I learned to do in my dancing and acting. When I was dancing, the choreographer would tell me what to do, and I would do it. When I was acting, the director would help me tailor my interpretation. Movies are a collaboration, but the director is unquestionably the boss. He knows what he wants, the feeling and tone of things. I went to work every day for years knowing that it was his ship and that I was lucky enough to be a sailor on it. I always kept a Goethe quote in mind: "It is within limits that the craftsman reveals himself." I was a craftsman. And believe me, there were always limits. I could work within them if I had to.

Around the time ABC started to air the first few episodes of *Good and Evil,* I was invited to the White House under the presidency of George H. W. Bush for a dinner to honor Violeta Barrios de Chamorro. I wasn't a huge fan of the Republican-run White House, but I had heard that the whole Chamorro family had been assassinated and that she was the new leader of Nicaragua. I was fascinated, having been raised in American schools, looking at the flag and the White House. Political pros and cons aside, I was going!

When I told Bob Morton, my old friend and Letterman's producer, that I was invited to the White House, he said, "You're takin' me." So I took Morty.

I bought a black sparkly Armani dress for the occasion, but in the hotel, as I was getting ready, I couldn't figure out how to button it. You had to be a rocket scientist to wear that dress. I made Morty come to my room to help, but he couldn't figure it out, either. Morty ended up calling the store in L.A. (I couldn't make the call because I was entangled in that dress like a fly in a spiderweb.) The store had to walk us through the buttoning of the dress like ground control guiding the *Apollo 13* astronauts back to Earth, but the result was great. I was perfectly wrapped and ready to present myself to the president.

At the White House we met the Bushes, the Quayles—the whole gang. It was a state dinner for a hundred people, all fancy with beautiful flowers and place cards. I went to my table, which was a table for ten. I looked at the place cards and said, "Oh my God! I'm sitting at the table with the president!" Michael Eisner (the real president of our country) was also at my table, as was the guest of honor herself.

The first thing I did when I sat down was turn over my plate to see who made it. I couldn't help it. President Bush caught me in the act, but he graciously said, "This was the set of dishes from the Kennedy White House. Every presidency gives a gift to the White House, and Jackie picked these out." I liked them. Jackie and I always had the same taste—at least in plates and men.

I looked around the table to see if I recognized anyone else. Everyone looked important but completely unfamiliar. Great. I turned to the stranger on my left, whose place card said his name was Ernie Ervin, and said, "Hi. Nice to meet you"—small talk, small talk—"What do you do?"

He said with a drawl, "I'm a race-car driver." At this point I really started to wonder what the criteria was to be invited to this dinner, and to sit with the president, no less. I said, "This is pretty exciting, that we're here at the White House, isn't it?"

Ernie said, "I know. I got this invitation and I thought it said 'steak dinner' at the White House." I just stared at him. He said, "I don't see any steak, but this is fine I guess." Actually, we were having poached salmon in champagne aspic with caviar sauce, something I make at home all the time.

As dessert was served, the president said to me, "I understand you're doing a new TV series." A lightbulb went on in my head. I had been invited to the White House by one of my agents at CAA, Bill Haber. And he was the one who'd set up the whole *Good and Evil* project. *Good and Evil* was going to be on ABC, ABC was owned by Disney, and Michael Eisner (as I said, the real president) was sitting at my table. I figured out that the president was in tight with Disney and ABC, and that's probably why I was there. So it wasn't exactly a dinner honoring my lifetime achievements as an actress. It wasn't that George and Barbara were big fans of Letterman, as I had suspected; it was all business. The important part of this revelation was that big money and big business will always be in tight with big politics. Where, I thought, does the little guy, the ordinary wage-earning American, fit into this picture? He doesn't. But enjoy the sorbet.

After dinner, which included strolling violin players, a voice came over the loudspeaker and said, "Please adjourn to the East Wing." As I stood up to go, President Bush said to me, "Why don't you take those matches there? Give 'em to your grandkids." (How sweet. I wonder if Jefferson did that when he had guests. "Here, take this candle wax.") Anyway, I took the souvenirs from the White House, and I still have them, soon to be available on eBay, perhaps. I thought to myself, Old George Bush is just an ordinary guy when it comes to souvenirs. Maybe he was a real person just like me who worried about leftovers and flat tires. Then I realized, He's the damn president of the United States; he has the power to do everything from send people to war, to make labor unions buckle under, to improve the quality of life for the poor and disabled, and a lot of other (hopefully positive) things. No, maybe we weren't that much alike, but it was nice to recognize a little common thread. I was looking for comfort in that. He also hates broccoli, which I found curiously refreshing, as I'm not that crazy about it myself.

The question (or enigma) of government has always loomed in my head. Yes, I studied it in school, but I never saw the actual connection between me and all those buildings in Washington. I, like a lot of other people, was just taught to revere and respect whatever politicians said or did. It seemed to be working pretty well as I was growing up, so I didn't pay much attention to the workings of Washington. I had other fish to fry, what with my theatrical aspirations and all. We were living in the greatest country on the planet. I didn't need to spend any energy worrying about governmental matters.

Then, in the '60s, with the invasion of Vietnam, things started to get a little cloudy for my generation. After figuring out that my one little vote didn't mean that much in the great scheme of things, I, along with many of my peers, became a grassroots activist. It seemed to be the only way to have a voice in anything. Even though my brother Ed was in Vietnam, I still thought it was wrong for us to be horning in over there. I attended lots of sit-ins and peace marches. Once I was even arrested (with César Chávez, one of my heroes) in Mercury, Nevada, at a nuclear dump site.

More and more I just didn't see how people could look at some-thing unjust and unfair and not try to do something about it. Eventually, I looked around at some of my fellow protesters, who were often labeled "The Lunatic Fringe," and realized that there might be a better way to go about making changes. I just wasn't sure how. Also, I figured out that it wasn't my job. Still, to this day, my disgruntlement with the government is a frustration. How can a person be a decent American and not speak out?

So, years later, there I was in Washington, rubbing elbows with the Bushes. I went from sitting on a bus in handcuffs to cleansing my palate at the White House. If that isn't full circle, I don't know what is.

I walked to the East Wing with Sylvester Stallone, who looked at a sculpture and said, "Hey, look, there's a Remington. You think it's real?" I said, "We're in the White House, Rocky. Of course it's real!" (But, actually, I wasn't so sure. I just wanted Stallone to think I knew more than he did.) We ended the evening lis-tening to Johnny Mathis sing "Chances Are," "Misty," and "Twelfth of Never." I liked the music. It was Barbara's choice and I thought, How romantic she is. I had something in common with her, too . . . not a lot, but something.

Good and Evil first aired in September 1991 and last aired in October 1991. They ran four of the thirteen episodes we shot. I was surprised they took it off so fast. From all the fanfare and preparation, I had assumed it would be my job for the next few years. All that hoopla for four half-hours of comedy. Canceled. After all that press saying "Teri Garr comes to TV after all these years," I was embarrassed to have the show disappear so quickly. You think government is confusing, try figuring out why TV shows fail. No, don't—it's a waste of time. I decided it wasn't my fault and let it go.

It was after the cancellation of that show that my limp took up permanent residence. In fact, let me blame *Good and Evil* for making me limp—one thing about having an infirmity is that you can always blame it on the thing you're mad at, at the time.

18

Brace Yourself

After *Good and Evil* my limp was just . . . there. It happened so gradually that I barely noticed it, but one day I got up to get a glass of water and realized that it took me forever to cross the room. It's not like I was in pain, it was just that it took extra energy to get my right foot off the ground. Gravity seemed to have a stronger pull on that foot, and it suddenly felt like it weighed fifty pounds. My walk changed. You know how it feels when your legs are really tired after spending all day chasing your kids or shopping and you'd rather not move? That's how I felt *all* the time. Life became less convenient. And people started noticing it more. I remembered that the actor Art Carney used to limp. When anyone asked him what was wrong, he would gruffly reply, "War injury," and walk on. I started saying that, too. After all, I was injured in the sexual revolution. (And quite badly, I might add.) I was still working here and there, though. At one point I was hired to do a commercial in Canada for cough syrup. When I arrived they told me they wanted me to roller-skate across the park with a little boy. Apparently, that was the image they felt would best communicate how healthy and active this cough syrup would make you feel. There was no way I could roller-skate; my days as the roller-skating Statue of Liberty were long past. But I didn't admit it. Instead, I said, "That's not a good idea. Too much movement." I noticed that there was a swing in the park. To distract everyone from their concept, I sat on the swing and started singing to the little boy, "Oh, the wheels on the bus go round and round." Next thing I knew, they shot the ad with the two of us on the swing. It was a wrap, and there was no mention of my limp.

Then, in 1992, I went to do a TV movie in Utah called *Deliver Them from Evil: The Taking of Alta View*. It was a true story about a guy, played by Harry Hamlin, who took hostages in the maternity ward of a hospital because his wife couldn't have kids and he blamed a doctor. Yeah, I know what you're thinking: "How many 'guy-who-takes-hostages-in-the-maternity-ward-because-his-wife-couldn't-have-kids-and-he-blamed-a-doctor' movies does the world need?" Apparently, a lot. Anyway, I played the head nurse who got taken hostage. At one point the director, Peter Levin, who had years of experience directing everything on TV from *Lou Grant* to *Law & Order*, said to me, "You know, you're limping."

I said, "No, I'm not." By that point, whenever anyone asked if I was limping, I would say, "No, I'm not," because that usually ended the conversation quicker than, "I was injured in the sexual revolution."

But Peter was a very nice and very direct man. He said, "Yeah, you are. It's a little noticeable." He was very practical about it. He said, "We'll just add a line in one of these scenes. The nurse will say, 'Why are you limping?' And you'll say, 'Oh, I was in a skiing

accident last week.' " I must have looked skeptical, but he continued. "Then it'll be done. So if people watch the show and say,
'Why is she limping?' the answer will be 'Remember the scene
where she said she had a skiing accident?' " So that's what we did.
It was as simple as that. I liked Peter Levin and was grateful for
his no-nonsense attitude. Someone limps, put a line in the
script—no big deal. I decided I would suggest something similar
if anyone noticed it again, on a later project.

But once I was off the set, it *was* a big deal. I'd be shopping, or
walking to my car, or crossing a restaurant to meet a tableful of
friends, and I'd stumble. Often I fell. Once I was hurrying down
the stairs to answer the phone and I fell and broke my collarbone.
Too bad I missed that call; maybe it was Jonathan Demme calling
to offer me Jodie Foster's role in *The Silence of the Lambs*.

I went to a doctor at UCLA about my now full-fledged limp.
He said, "Let me see you walk." I walked up and down the hall
outside his office, and he said, "It looks like you've developed drop
foot. I think you could walk better if you supported your foot with
a brace." I was doubtful, but he fitted me for a leg brace, anyway.
About a week later, I went back to his office. The brand-new brace
was an elegant flesh-colored plastic support that ran up the back of
my calf like a long shoehorn. I put it on my foot, put my shoe on,
and started walking. It was fabulous! My leg felt lighter and easier
to lift. I could move much faster. I felt like I'd just checked my bags
and was free to walk around the airport. I was strolling along just
like the old days. It was the greatest thing I had felt, seen, or done
in a long time. Then the doctor said, "You know, you'll have to
wear long skirts or pants if you don't want it to show.

I blurted out, "You mean you're telling me, Teri Garr, known
primarily for my great legs, that I have to cover them up?" He

looked at me and said, "That's a small price to pay to walk better, isn't it?" Hmm. Tough decision, but he was right. It *is* a small price to pay. I figured I could compensate for the lack of leg by being more, shall we say, charming and witty. But it was a blow to my vanity.

The brace changed my life in terms of how I felt about walking. And in case you ever take walking for granted: *Don't.* Take it from me. Not for a single second. I can walk around the block, but it's hardly effortless. It's exhausting. I miss effortless walking more than anything. (No, that's not true—I miss effortless dishwashing, too.)

I was worried that the limp would put an end to my career. The unconfirmed gossip of a few years prior had finally faded away. I'd done a really silly movie with Jon Lovitz called *Mom and Dad Save the World* and several TV movies, and I thought that made it clear that rumors of my incapacity had been greatly exaggerated. But now, ironically, just as the rumors were slowing down, and I was dealing with my symptoms, a real disability emerged: prejudice.

Soon after, I went to work on *Adventures in Wonderland*, a Disney series based on *Alice's Adventures in Wonderland*. I played the Duchess, and the part required that I dance. I had no problem with the dancing; I just led with my left foot, and my limp disappeared. But one day it was really hot and I took off my brace to give my leg a little air. We shot a scene, and then the director said, "Cut! Someone's leg is in the scene. It's on the floor. We have to shoot it again."

I said, "Oh, that would be mine." I'd taken off my shoe and left my brace in the shot. (I'm not responsible for the damn thing if it's not on my leg.)

People were equally accepting in my next sitcom, *Good Advice*. It starred Shelley Long as a marriage counselor who shared office space with a divorce lawyer played by Treat Williams. The producer wanted to spice things up by adding me to the cast to play Shelley's (younger, more beautiful) sister. I was game. The scripts were funny and I loved the executive producer, Michael Patrick King, who'd written for *Murphy Brown* and would go on to *Sex and the City* fame; and Tom Palmer, a funny showrunner who'd also written for *Murphy Brown*.

I'll never forget when I went in to meet with them for the first time. I was at a point where I was sick of people asking me about my limp. I said, "I have to wear long skirts because I have a brace on my leg." Michael replied, "Yeah, yeah, whatever. Let's read this comedy gold and see what happens." Finally, someone in show business was seeing it like I did. His feeling was, if you're a funny actress, you're a funny actress, and limping is the least of your worries. I loved him for that.

The brace did wonders for my limp, but I was still feeling a little tired sometimes. All I wanted to do was sleep. One of my doctors put me in a hot tub—only in California, right? I don't know what he thought would come of it, and I didn't ask. Obeying random doctor commands was my favorite hobby at the time. I figured his next suggestion was going to be that I juggle while he observed. When I stepped out of the steaming water, I was physically drained. The doctor took one look at me and said, "This might be MS." I had heard MS from doctors before, but I had never heard it mentioned so definitively. (Except from the press, and the last time I checked, they hadn't been to medical school.) This time, for some reason, it sank in. Multiple sclerosis. MS. But come on! After so many doctors, so many tests, and no diagnoses, how was I supposed to believe this guy? So I didn't believe him—yet. Anyway, he wasn't sure. But I did pay attention. I knew that none of those diseases with initials were good, but if one of them was the answer to my mystery symptoms, I definitely wanted to know about it.

So I took matters into my own hands. I started researching MS. The best technical definition I came up with was that MS is an autoimmune disease in which immune-system cells, known as T cells, begin to destroy the fatty substance that coats and insulates nerve fibers in the brain and spinal cord. The breakdown of this substance, called myelin, disrupts the transmission of electric signals from the brain, causing such symptoms as fatigue, muscle weakness, heat sensitivity, loss of balance, difficulty walking, and slurred speech. Huh. Blah, blah, blah. Okay, I thought, fatigue, heat sensitivity—I could actually be in the ballpark here.

The way I like to describe it is this: You know when you see a bunch of multicolored electric wires all twisted together and covered with black rubber? Well, the colored wires are like your nerves, and the black rubber is like the myelin sheath that protects them. If you have MS, your body attacks itself, so the myelin sheath (the black rubber) slowly gets destroyed. The holes cause communication breakdown. When people with MS have an exacerbation, *boom*: pins and needles, beeping, fatigue, weakness, and in extreme episodes you might think O. J. Simpson is still going to track down Nicole's murderer—unlikely, but possible.

Most people have relapsing-remitting MS, which means that after an attack, they go into a period of remission that can last for years. About 15 percent of people with MS have progressive MS, which doesn't go into remission—it just gets worse at different rates of progression, depending on the person.

I could relate to plenty of the MS symptoms, but the more research I did, the more horrific stories I heard. And then my episode faded away. I stopped feeling weak and tired. I still had to wear my brace, but otherwise I felt perfectly fine. When I felt better, I put the research away. I didn't want to think about being sick when I felt well. It was easier to put it on the back burner. Until the words "You have MS" came out of the mouths of professionals, I didn't want to entertain the thought.

Besides, my mind was on family matters and, just to keep you interested, sex. You heard me.

19

Coming in for a Landing

A couple years before *Good Advice,* I did the play *Love Letters* with the sweet, funny, handsome, and wonderful Robert Urich at the Canon Theater in Beverly Hills. The play essentially consists of the correspondence between a man and a woman who are pen pals for life. (It's a pretty rehearsal-light play, since all you have to do is read the letters to each other onstage.) One night, my friend Heidi told me that she was going to bring a friend to the play, a guy she wanted me to meet. It had been a few months since my charge of the hammer brigade, and I was cautiously optimistic about dating. So Heidi brought John O'Neil to the play, and they came backstage. I saw this very handsome Irishman walk in the door. I pointed to him and said, "Are you for me?" He was. We made plans to go out for coffee after the play.

I told Robert Urich that I was excited about my blind date after the show. He said, "Whatever you do, *don't* tell him the break-the-windows-of-the-ex story." I never stop telling people that

194

story. I kept hoping someone would tell me why, why, why this terrible thing had happened to me, the Queen of America. I'm actually surprised I didn't tell George Bush about it. "How do you do, Mr. President? Let me just tell you this story about my old boyfriend. Not interested? Maybe Barbara is? I hear she's a romantic." I told that story every chance I got. I wasn't much for discretion.

So John waited for me after the play, and we went to a nearby Beverly Hills restaurant for a nightcap. Within the first hour I told him the bang-bang-Teri's-silver-hammer story, and instead of running for shelter, he tried to top it with his own story. He told me that he was a pilot, and when he was living with one of his girlfriends he used to fly over their house. He would see a truck in the driveway. The first time, he thought nothing of it. The second time, he started to get suspicious. Indeed, she was cheating on him with a guy who drove a brand-new Dodge Ram pickup. He didn't succumb to vandalism; he just broke up with her.

The next day I was at home when he called to say, "I'm above your house in my plane. I'm going to Catalina." I looked up at the sky. There wasn't a plane in sight, but I waved up at the empty blue sky, anyway. After my complicated relationship with David and my disastrous interlude with S*#T, John seemed very uncomplicated. He was a sweet teddy bear with a good heart— and a college education, a car, a house, a career as a contractor, and an airplane. He looked good on paper. He had his own life. I was intrigued.

John and I started dating. He was kind of a macho outdoorsman, and together we did things I'd never done before. We took his plane to see the Anasazi cliff dwellings in Canyon de Chelly. He landed on a dirt road and we hitchhiked to a hotel. We flew from L.A. to Seattle at five hundred feet, staying on the coast the whole way. We'd stop at little towns along the way and explore, but flying that plane was like being in a garbage can. It shook and rattled and eventually I decided I'd rather be on the ground, waving up at it. But we took hikes—with my brace I was a new woman—and explored together. John didn't like to go to parties. I didn't mind; I didn't like parties that much myself. I was happy for an excuse to stay home. We went to bed early and got up early. And John couldn't have cared less about my leg brace. In fact, he thought it was sexy. I thought, This could be serious.

Most of all, John shared my desire for a family. Yes, this was really very important to me, and time was closing in. I was over forty, and as in the past, I just wasn't getting pregnant, but we kept trying. We did all sorts of romantic things like taking fertility shots, having emergency sex, and dashing jars of sperm off to the doctor. Very kinky. Soon, I became frustrated and depressed. I'd spent so many years on my career, making sure I didn't miss the boat like my father had. Had the baby boat sailed right past me in the meantime? It was John who finally suggested adoption. After all the futility of fertility, that sounded good to me. We heard about "open adoption," where you register with a lawyer and the mothers call you to talk, essentially interviewing potential parents for their babies. They can talk to you as many times as they like before deciding who they want to adopt their children. It was like an audition! And I didn't even have to pretend to be someone else. I could handle that.

I talked to two women, and the second one liked me. I told her that I was an actress (we only used first names, but I don't think she would have heard of me, anyway) and that my husband was a building contractor. (Husband was a bit of an overstatement, but we would deal with that later.) The mother lived in Austin, Texas, and was feisty and independent. Good. The next thing I knew, the lawyer from the adoption office called me to say, "Okay, she is four months along, and she would like you to take her baby when it's born." John and I were both really excited. I may have come late to the family game, but it was all happening for me at once: A husband-to-be, a baby-to-be—a family of my own. I couldn't wait for Thanksgiving dinners with noise and friends and family. I was mapping out my plan like it was a screenplay in which I would play the part of mom. I think that probably happens with a lot of people, but for me it was like, Is this really happening? I'd be bopping along with my day and suddenly remember, There's a baby coming. It didn't seem real.

I was working on *Good Advice* as our baby's birth approached. It was November, our baby was due at end of December, the mother was coming to Santa Monica for the birth, and we still weren't married. I presented a number of matrimonial options—I was attending a benefit in Aspen and thought we could get married in the library that weekend; same thing in San Francisco. But John kept getting cold feet. He had been divorced and wasn't sure he wanted to get married again. I didn't take him very seriously. Maybe I should have, but I was much too focused on carrying out my scenario.

On Thanksgiving weekend we decided to go to Cabo San Lucas, Mexico, just to get away. When we were checking in at the hotel, we saw a sign that read, CONCIERGE WILL MARRY YOU FOR $200. I said, "John, look! Let's go get married." He said, "Ooookaaaay." I had to drag him, but we went and filled out all the papers. On Saturday night, on the terrace of the hotel, we got married. Everyone at the hotel was very excited. The waiters were the witnesses and guests, and they swore they'd come back every year to celebrate our anniversary. I wore a white sundress I bought that day and carried a bouquet of wild Mexican flowers. John wore a blue shirt and black pants. We didn't look like *Weddings* magazine, but I have to say we looked pretty good. So on Saturday night at seven, just as the sun was setting, we tied the knot. The judge who married us did the whole ceremony in Spanish. After-ward I asked her to translate some of it. She said, "It says you will obey your husband and always follow behind him." Hmm, I thought, I don't think so.

When the festivities ended, John and I went back to our room. The hotel had spread a path of bougainvillea petals down the hall-way and into the room, culminating in a heart made of flower petals on the bed. I turned to John and said, "I can't believe I fi-nally talked you into this!" I had never had a white-wedding fan-tasy, and getting married on the spur of the moment suited me just fine. It was more practical than romantic, but I was glad it was done. I was calm and content. The baby was due in a month, and now we were ready. At least I thought we were.

The next day we returned home to Los Angeles, and we went to our respective houses. Yes, we were married, but we still didn't live together. One thing at a time. So we left the airport and John went to his house to get some stuff. As I was driving home, my car phone rang. It was John. He said, "The baby was born last night!"

"What baby?" I said. "Our baby?" I couldn't believe it. "Wow! Great! Is it a boy or a girl?"

He said, "It's a little girl, and we have to go pick her up."

"But where are we going to put her?" I asked. At this point we didn't have a crib, a diaper, anything. With my friend Bebe, John and I went to the hospital in Santa Monica to get her. John was a wreck when we picked her up. He tried to pay the doctors for the parking. She had been born three weeks early, so it was all very hectic and exciting. In the car on the way home, John and I were both talking at the same time. I wanted to name her Louise, but he didn't. We both wanted our aunts' names as her middle name. And in the backseat sat Molly (we finally agreed), a little eggplant, wondering who these crazy people were. There she was, cute as cute could be. She was twelve hours old and coming home with us!

I always tell Molly, "We were getting married at seven and you were born at eight! You were out there flying around in the cosmos and said, 'Okay, they're married, I'm coming in for a landing.'" She loves that story. At last, I had the family I'd wanted for so long. And even though I don't believe in psychic, new-age stuff, it was pretty special how it all came together, and I thank my lucky stars every day. I guess God, if She's out there, probably did orchestrate the whole thing.

After years of acting the part of wife and mother, I finally had my chance to be one. Not surprisingly, at that moment my life changed immediately and forever. I was late to work because now I had the baby. (Actually, I was always late to work, but now I had an excuse.)

My mother came to see Molly the first weekend, and that's when I realized that she was really starting to be a little off. She couldn't quite process the fact that we'd adopted Molly. She kept saying, "Look at you, up and about! I could barely walk after I had my children." She was genuinely impressed by my speedy recovery from childbirth. But no matter how out of it she was, she was wild about Molly. And she still managed to make her famous

Thanksgiving gravy, even though Thanksgiving was over. We took lots of videos of mom, the baby, the gravy, and the baby in the gravy. Remember, we're show people.

The first summer with Molly we rented a beach house on Balboa Island. It's a little island, south of L.A., that I'd been visiting since I was a kid. We'd put Molly in a stroller, take her down to the beach, and show her off to anyone who would pay attention. At night we'd rent movies and order pizza, or go out for Italian food. Our life was simple and we were happy. It was the first vacation I'd ever had where I wasn't worried about my next job. Toward the end of that summer, I remember sitting on the porch in the late afternoon while John lit up the barbecue. The sun was setting over the water right in front of us. I sat with Molly in my arms, smelling the charcoal lighter and watching sailboats more in and out of the harbor.

This was pretty damn good. In fact, it was enough.

Four years earlier it had seemed like I'd lost everything. My friends had betrayed my trust; my health wasn't great, and rumors about it were worse; my movie career had halted midstream; my boyfriend had cheated on me; and I wasn't sure what the future held. Still, everything was okay. Somehow I'd rebuilt my career through sheer force of will. I'd literally gotten the support of a leg brace. And John, Molly, and I were a small, happy family.

I never imagined the impact a child would have on my life. When she was a baby, Molly did the typical cute baby things but, to us (typical parents), they were the greatest things that ever happened to us. John and I used to look at each other and say, "We won the lottery!" She loved looking at herself in the "miro," and when I would be getting ready to go out, she'd ask me to dab her with "fear-fume" (translation: perfume; I thought this was rather appropriate, since she's been fearless since birth).

Once, when she was about seven, Molly was taking tennis lessons in L.A. and we ran into John McEnroe at the courts. I introduced her to him, telling him that she was an avid tennis student. "Great!" he said, "Let me see your backhand," at which point Molly showed him the back of her left hand. Perfect.

I'm sure most mothers say this, but *I* really mean it: My daughter is a wonderful human being, the greatest accomplishment of my life.

So far.

20

She's Up, She's Down, She's Up, She's Down

Soon after Molly was born I stopped going on Letterman's show. I'd been appearing a few times a year for about ten years starting in 1985, but by that point, things just weren't the same. It was now more difficult to drop everything and just jump on a plane. I had also started to feel like filler. I know I wasn't always Dave's first choice. I wasn't a stand-up comic. And I often didn't have anything to plug—not even a Vegomatic.

Whenever a celebrity goes on Letterman's show, the segment producer calls them to do a pre-interview. They talk about what stories they're going to tell on the show. After having been on the show hundreds of times, I started feeling like they should trust my ability to appear without being screened.

Once, just before Molly was born, I went to New York to do the show, and when the producer called, I wouldn't go over my planned topics. I used the excuse that I was an actress, damn it, and I wasn't responsible for writing special material for talk

202

shows. Looking back, I was wrong, I suppose. It must be really hard to plan, produce, and host one of those shows every night of the week. But there I was, cavalierly saying, "Oh, I don't need to talk to the segment producer about my spot, I'll just wing it." It must have driven them crazy, yet they were always polite. But I think sometimes Dave just looked at me and laughed because I was so unprepared. He must have thought, Is this woman nuts?

Of course, I never got away with that no-rehearsal thing with Carson. I always told them something. I once saw Angie Dickinson on *The Tonight Show* talking about worms in her driveway after the rain. I figured I could always talk about how I'm pretty sure my dog is psychic.

So, okay, looking back I can see that I wasn't being respectful. Once Steve Martin told me he spent two weeks working on material for his seven minutes with Letterman. I couldn't believe it, but he did, and he was right. I think deep down I was just scared that I wouldn't ever be as brilliant as they were, so why try at all? The truth is, I owe David Letterman a lot since he helped put me on the map.

And I'm not just saying that so he'll have me on to talk about this book. But he better.

Something else was also going on. Now I had a husband and a baby. I still wasn't feeling all that well, and I'd been cheerful and funny on demand for years. It had been a nonstop hustle. I needed to close down shop for a while, even if I didn't realize it. As a mother, I notice that when Molly doesn't want to do something, she becomes bad at it. When she loses interest, she turns apathetic, and her skills slip. Subconsciously, I must have been tired of doing that show. I guess I just wanted to be home. I wanted normal, whatever that is.

My nesting impulse didn't dissuade me from doing yet another television series at home in L.A. This one was called *Women of the House.* It was written by the Arkansas-bred friends of Bill Clinton, Harry Thomason and Linda Bloodworth-Thomason. They were well-known television people who had produced *Designing Women* and put together the Clinton documentary called *The Man from Hope* that aired at the Democratic National Convention in 1992. The Thomasons wanted to give a show about the women of the White House a shot. As someone who had dined at the White House, I felt more than qualified. The show starred Delta Burke, Patricia Heaton, and me.

I played an alcoholic press agent. I didn't give my limp a second thought; I thought the leg brace made it unnoticeable. But one day Delta Burke came up to me and said, "You bitter git yer story straight cuz everone is askin' 'bout you, and there are fifty different sturies out there." I was actually flattered that there were *any* stories out there. Every time I took a new job, the question of what exactly was causing my limp resurfaced. I didn't have a satisfying answer. It seemed foolish to stand up and say, "I don't know." As far as I knew, that was the truth. But six years earlier I had seen the toll that mere rumors of MS could take on my career. I saw no point in confirming something that remained unconfirmed—not to mention that I really felt that what was going on in my body was nobody's business.

When we were promoting *Women of the House,* I did an interview with *TV Guide.* It was supposed to be about how the show related to *Mr. Smith Goes to Washington.* At some point in the interview the journalist asked me, "Do you have MS?"

I said, "Not that I know of. But I'd rather talk about the show." That was it. No problem. But when the article came out, it was all about my health. It said, "Teri Garr says she doesn't have MS," and went into detail about the way I walk, the brace, and so on. I don't know why I was so surprised. Gossip sells magazines; I know that. But it was such a tiny part of a much longer interview devoted to a completely different topic, and I had trusted the journalist. I'd never had to watch what I said to the press before. I probably should have.

Now people started to come up to me to say, "You'll feel much better if you come out and say what you have." But I didn't know what I had. I wasn't going to "come out" about my assorted collection of mysterious symptoms that sometimes were there and sometimes were not. I feared the damage to my career, and I resented the intrusion. Oh God, why hadn't I just been an upholsterer? But friends, colleagues, everyone seemed unsatisfied. If I was going to limp in public, on camera, they wanted to know why. *Women of the House* lasted only one season. I guess alcoholic political career women just aren't that interesting. And don't forget, we never know what makes a series stay on the air; it's an enigma. Check out Charlie Sheen in *2½ Dads*. I rest my case, your honor.

In 1997, I did a few episodes of *Friends*, playing Phoebe's mom. I honestly never thought I would see the day where I played the mother of someone in her thirties. I'm not sure I resemble Lisa Kudrow, but she is such a nice, talented person that if I had given birth at the tender age of, say, ten, I would have loved for her to be my daughter. Molly was curious about the show. She asked me if Lisa Kudrow was her sister, and I tried to explain the magic of television to my four-year-old. Then she came to a taping and had to go through security. They asked her what her name was, and she said, "I'm Molly O'Neil, Teri Garr's daughter. Her *only* daughter."

Aside from *Friends,* I was pretty much "between engagements," as we say in the provinces. I loved my home life, but the push-push-push of the earlier years didn't disappear overnight, so I set up a meeting at William Morris, thinking that if I met face-to-face with my agents, it would reignite their interest in me. It wouldn't be the first time I'd had to put someone back on the right track. These people were supposed to be working for me. At the meeting they were pleasant, and then one of them said, "I heard it's not just your foot that is weak. I heard it's your hand, too." Then he said, "Let me see your hand." I was about ready to call this kid's mother; where were his manners? But I made a joke of it and walked out of there thinking, I don't think they get it. Surely I'd reminded them that I was employable.

A few years later, my manager called and announced that he had set up a meeting for me with a director, David O. Russell. In Hollywood-speak, that means the director had hunted me down. He had done a few great movies—*Spanking the Monkey, Flirting with Disaster,* and *Three Kings*—and he was interested in me for his new project, *I ♥ Huckabees.* I liked his work and was curious to meet the auteur.

The meeting was held at a little house up in the Santa Monica mountains that had been rented as a production office. After almost getting lost on traversing roads, I finally found it. I always look for the best parking—meaning the spot that makes it easiest to get from my car to the door—so I parked in the driveway at the back of the house. I walked around to the front and knocked on the door. When the door opened, there stood a youngish, good-looking director type with brown shoulder-length rocker hair, dressed in khakis and a grungy T-shirt. When he saw me, he fell to his knees in campy worship and gushed, "Oh my God! Look who's here!" I was flattered. Then he said, "Let me carry you! Let me carry you in!" I said, "No, I'm fine, I can walk." But despite my protests, he grabbed me below the knees and carried me over the threshold. It was awkward at best.

David O. Russell carried me into the living room and invited me to sit down. I noticed a huge poster of Bob Dylan and some photographs of people like Yves Saint Laurent. I thought, Very hip, very eclectic.

After about twenty minutes he reemerged from his office and sat a good six inches from my face. He said, "Do you know how much I love you? Do you know how much all your work has meant to me?" I laughed and thanked him. I thought about the old days, before the Elvis movies, when I couldn't get arrested, and how I really do appreciate it when people genuinely respond to my work. David O. Russell told me his script was about a guy "evaluating the spirituality of his feelings and his life in an existential way." Okay. Then he asked, "Do you understand what I mean?"

I didn't have a clue but couched my ignorance by smiling sweetly and saying, "Not exactly." I was hoping he'd say, "This movie is about an older woman who has huge sex appeal, and you'd be great for the part because you are hot, hot, hot." But I digress. He went on to say, "If a person suddenly contracted, oh, MS, for example . . . how would it affect them? How would they deal with it?" I was taken aback, but I let it pass. I figured he was trying to give an example that I would understand.

So I just said, "Sure, sure, I understand, you mean dealing with alternatives. I can do the job. What's the part?" He picked up the script and read a scene about a conventional couple sitting at a dinner table with their two children and their adopted African son. He wanted me for the part of the mother. I thought it was hilarious. I said, "When does it shoot?"

He looked at the schedule and said, "Three days in June." I thought, Three days in June? Well, it certainly isn't a very big part, but it is pretty juicy, so I'm in. I really hoped he wanted me to do it. Then he peered at me and slowly said, "You just want to get this job and get the hell out of here, don't you?" I said, "No, no. Let's talk." But then he said, "You're nothing like you are on Letterman, are you?" What the hell was he talking about? Some young directors who have seen me in movies or on television want to meet me. They have this image in their head, an image they've created which isn't me, sort of like Ingrid Bergman in *Casablanca*. I no longer had faith that he was really considering me for the part. And now, he was right—all I wanted to do was get out of there. After a few minutes I said, "I'll read your script. I'd love to do the part. I'm gonna go now."

He said, "Okay."

I said, "Do you have a back door so I don't have to walk down those stairs?"

He replied, "Here, let me carry you."

I thought, Oh no. Please, just show me where the back door is. But I said, "No. That's okay." But he wouldn't take no for an answer. He and his cowriter put their shoulders under my armpits and dragged me across the room. This had never happened to me before. I may drag my foot, but I've always been able to get across a room. I didn't know whether to stop them or play along with their silly charade. And I was taken so off-guard that I had no idea how to stop it.

I was never so glad to get to my car in my life. And I never heard from him again. Just like his movie, that meeting made me "evaluate the spirituality of my feelings and my life in an existential way." Now I get it. We lived out the essence of the movie in the meeting. Now I don't even have to see it.

Ever since I saw *The Music Man,* I've had a fantasy about living in River City, Iowa. I love the idea of a place where nice people live on tree-lined streets with houses that have porches and rocking chairs. On Sunday morning in Hollywood, people read *Variety* or take their kids to a birthday party for a two-year-old that has live chimps, catering, and costs $10,000. In my fantasy of River City, Iowa, people go to church on Sunday. And if someone in River City, Iowa, were to come down with a devastating disease, a neighbor would bake a pie for them, maybe offer to help them out. No big deal. They would wish their neighbors health and happiness. Life would be simple. (Of course, they might also have voted George W. into office. Somebody did, and it sure wasn't me.)

I know it's only a city girl's fantasy of Middle America, but it helps me to believe that place exists. I have a friend in upstate New York who teaches school. He recently told me about a fellow teacher who was diagnosed with MS. He said, "The only difference is that he had to go from head soccer coach to assistant soccer coach because he gets tired." No one treats him differently. I wish it could be like that everywhere, I thought. Maybe I should think about coaching soccer.

But I don't live in River City, Iowa, or in upstate New York. I live in L.A., and, obviously, something is off. At that time, my view of myself wasn't jiving with the way others saw me, and it was creating friction everywhere I went. I always downplayed my disease, whatever it was. By nature and philosophy, my response was to ignore it. This worked for me, though it clearly didn't work for the rest of the world.

My friendships and business relationships may have been imperfect, but what was most important was that John, Molly, and I were a family. On Friday nights when Molly was a baby there was a show on called *Picket Fences* about a *Twin Peaks*–esque town in Wisconsin. I decided that Molly loved that show. So while John read nearby, I'd walk back and forth in the living room holding Molly, all of us watching *Picket Fences*. I was happy to be with her, happy to be in bed by ten o'clock. Whenever I was working I took Molly with me if I could. Once, she and John came to Hawaii with me for a charity golf tournament. We stayed at one of the resort hotels. We ate in the same restaurant every night. When they saw us coming they'd spread plastic across the floor surrounding our table. Molly was apparently a little Jackson Pollock, squishing mashed potatoes and peas all over the floor. I was proud to see such talent at such an early age.

My life with John and Molly was worth everything. I knew if I had a bad day I would go home and there would be this sweet little thing waiting there, just for me. I was crazy about her. My increasingly complicated relationships in Hollywood and with my disease were less important when I woke up in the morning to see Molly's smiling, innocent face.

Much to my utter astonishment and disbelief, I realized I could be happy without pushing for my career all the time.

21

Elvis Has Left the Building

In the late '90s I took a renewed interest in MS. It was about time. I stopped caring what the doctors did or didn't know and could or couldn't tell me. I decided that knowledge was the best answer I could give myself. I went to one of Nancy Davis's "Race to Erase MS" seminars. Nancy is my generous and philanthropic friend, who happens to have MS, and who happens to be in with the very-in crowd (she comes from the family on whom Aaron Spelling loosely based *Dynasty*). She is a great motivator and has decided to put her time and energy into fighting MS. Her organization, Center Without Walls, funds neurologists, scientists, and clinicians to find not just a cure, but also innovative approaches to dealing with MS. In short, she supports the brilliant mad scientists who believe they can change the world of MS as we know it by rallying celebrities and others to the cause.

The doctors and researchers funded by Center Without Walls meet about four times a year to trade ideas and information. And every year Nancy has a huge benefit auction with lots of movie stars and models. Tommy Hilfiger, whose sister has MS, puts on a fashion show. It's a Hollywood extravaganza worth the razzle-dazzle because she raises more than a million dollars a year.

The morning after a huge fund-raiser I went with my friend Henriette Mantel to a seminar where all the neurologists lined up onstage to talk about MS. Henriette and I became friends when she played Shelley Long's nanny/housekeeper on *Good Advice*. Eight years after that, she was diagnosed with MS. Henriette was the first real friend I had with MS, and being able to compare notes with her changed the way I saw the disease. At the MS seminar, Henriette and I sat together and eyed the lineup of neurologists as if they were prize cattle. When we heard Dr. Leslie Weiner speak we said, "We want that one!"

Dr. Weiner is chairman and professor of neurology at the USC School of Medicine, where he's been teaching since 1975. In spite of his formidable credentials, he was more of a rumpled, mad scientist than the rest, and we liked that. Henriette said, "We have to go to this guy." We approached him. He gave us his number but said, "I'm in the middle of taking a year off from my practice to do an experiment." What? How dare he take a year off to help four hundred thousand people with MS and probably win a Nobel Prize for medicine when this Oscar-nominated actress needed attention *now*! I called his office, anyway, but his assistant told me to call back in July, when he would be seeing regular patients. I dutifully marked the calendar for July and made an appointment.

That appointment changed my life. I spent the month before gathering all my records from all the doctors who'd ever seen me. My dining room looked like a crime-scene investigation, with files and X-rays spread out in neat piles. After shipping him the records, the tests, the MRI results, my high-school grade point average, and my last five years of tax returns, Dr. Weiner was the first to say, "This is probably MS." The next thing out of his mouth was, "Let's get you on some drug therapy, ASAP." I'd seen on the Internet that there were several therapies available, and I'd wondered why I wasn't on one. It was because this was the first real diagnosis I'd had. Yes, here was a proactive doctor who wanted to move forward with treatment—treatment other than ropes and pulleys, Valium, and transcendental meditation. In all my years of going to doctors, not one of them had ever put me on any medicine that was specifically designed to treat MS. I couldn't wait to try it.

People always ask, "What was it like when you got the diagnosis? Was it shocking? Did you cry? Did you fall down in a dead faint?" All I can say is no. Every time I went to doctors, as you may have noticed, it was this and that, maybe it's MS, maybe it's not. So by the time I got an official MS diagnosis from Dr. Weiner, it was anything but traumatic. After twenty years of doctors saying, "You're imagining things," it was a relief to finally have someone say, "This is what it is; let's deal with it."

For many people, this is not the case. Often people experience shock, depression, fear, and denial. Plenty of people go through all the stages of realization in quick succession. Not me. My diagnosis had taken years, so I was glad to finally have one. It gave me a starting point. But it didn't make sense to call my friends and family. Why worry everybody? They would only let their imaginations run wild. But I knew the quest was over. Dr. Weiner said, "The Chinese word for crisis contains two characters, one meaning danger and the other meaning opportunity." I had a fifty-fifty chance.

The first drug he put me on was Betaseron. It turned out that I was very allergic to it. I learned right away that all drugs aren't for everyone. You have to customize them to fit your own needs. Like putting whitewalls on an old Chevy, sometimes it works and sometimes it doesn't.

Next he put me on Rebif, another form of interferon that slows the progression of MS. I inject Rebif three times a week into my stomach or leg or butt. I'm sure it's helping me because I feel better and have fewer lesions on my MRIs. In fact, my last MRI showed no lesions. Who knows how it would look if I weren't on medication? I'm not about to take that gamble. I'll leave the gambling to my father's ghost.

Now that I officially had MS, I decided to take a closer look at what was on the Internet. Some of the things I read were not that pretty. I came across a lot of descriptive words—*devastating, debilitating, weakening, chronic*—but the one that really didn't sit too well was *degenerative*. (Maybe they were describing that last series I did with Shelley Long? Now *that* was debilitating.) I decided to go back to my show-business roots and look at the bright side of things. MS can be surprising, inventive, and often inspiring. I started saying, "I may have MS, but I have the best MS in town." I felt better when I said it like that.

I always strive to be the best at whatever I do. Sometimes people like to remind me that MS is a progressive disease. Right after I say, "Thank you for sharing that slice of positivity," I say, "You know what? *Life* is a progressive disease. In fact, life is the leading cause of death. We're all doomed. Ain't none of us getting out of this alive!" See, I choose to believe that life is full of good things: creative people; happy families; chocolate; loyal friends; inspiring

children; and, of course, the Beatles. MS is just a speedbump . . .
a little one.

Dr. Weiner is a scientist and a hard worker. He was recently
written up in the *Los Angeles Times* for researching a vaccine for
MS. That research is the experiment that he was starting when I
first tried to meet with him. He is trying to create a vaccine for MS
patients that would prevent further nerve damage. Essentially, it
would teach our immune systems to fight our own bad T cells—
the cells that are attacking the myelin sheath (remember? that
black rubber tube?). No new lesions would form, and MS would
be halted in its tracks. Dr. Weiner gives me hope. I hope his experiment works. I hope he makes us all better. I hope the guy gets
the Nobel Prize for Science, and I hope that when he receives it he
wears a dress by Frabrice that makes him look like Joe Namath.

A while ago I was talking to my friend Buck Henry on the
phone, telling him about giving speeches, and he said, "Damn, I
wish I had a disease to exploit." I laughed and said, "Is that what
I'm doing?" But as far as I was concerned, it was a one-way relationship, and MS was exploiting me.

Soon after that conversation, I ran into David Lander
(Squiggy). David was first diagnosed with MS in 1984, when he
was thirty-seven. He didn't go public with his diagnosis until
1999. David thought it would be good for me to talk about my experience. By taking a public stance, he said, I could make people
feel better. I'd show them that they weren't alone. Since I was taking the drug Rebif, the company that makes it, Serono, asked me
if I wanted to be an ambassador for MS LifeLines, an educational
support service they sponsor. Hmm. Ambassador. Would I get to
wear a cape and crown? They said I could if I wanted to, but what

they really wanted was for me to travel around the country and talk about my experiences living with MS. They said it might make people feel better if they saw someone up there functioning in spite of the fact that they have this debilitating—blah, blah, blah—disease. I wasn't so sure. It didn't make sense to talk about my symptoms. What was I going to tell people: "Sometimes I feel good, but sometimes I don't"? Who doesn't have ups and downs? But the cat was out of the bag, anyway. Elvis had left the building. If I could help one person—not a Hollywood agent, a *real* person—it might be worth it. If I could figure out a way to find humor in this scum-sucking pig of a disease (and I mean that in the nicest way possible), then maybe it was time for me to step forward.

I was attached to my privacy, and I wasn't sure I wanted to make MS part of my public identity. MS is tricky. It encourages you to ignore it. As I've said, it took years before a neurologist or doctor ever said to me, "You have MS." So I had nothing to report. I was living my life the way I wanted to. I didn't want my disease to be a defining part of who I was, Teri Garr = MS.

Eventually, I realized that maybe helping other people feel better was a better idea than preserving my fragile acting career, which was being sidetracked by the old rumor mill, anyway. I didn't know until later that helping other people would make me feel better, too. But I had never actually made a public statement. I was afraid that if I announced my disease, I'd be in for a whole new round of discrimination. People in show business always have to protect themselves from rumors, truths, and undiagnosed diseases alike. At one of my doctors' offices, many patients are Hollywood people—producers, agents, and network executives. They have been diagnosed with Parkinson's, MS, Huntington's—

all the hip, trendy neurological diseases. They use fake names and pay the bills in cash without using their insurance because they don't want it to come out that anything is wrong with them. These are the same people who are in positions to decide whether to hire me. Ironic, right? They are afraid that their own physical problems will affect their ability to be hired. So what, dear God, must they think of me? And they are people who work with their brains (well, in theory, anyway) instead of their bodies.

There are endless stories of people whose work lives were compromised by MS. It happens all around us, all the time. A man with MS came up to me once and said that when he told his boss he had MS, his boss fired him. The boss even wrote in a memo: "I'm firing you because you have MS." His lawyer called this "The Golden Memo." He sued for two million dollars and won. It's different in Hollywood. The doors just quietly close. They say, "We decided to go another way."

Public knowledge of my disease could do more than dry up my career opportunities. The unsolicited medical advice would come from every corner—friends, fans, family, acquaintances. People struggle with how to react to illness, and I think it's part of human nature to overrespond, whether with undue pity, discrimination, or just plain wackiness. "My friend put magnets in the mattress and, next thing you know, she wasn't limping." Or, "My sister ate orange peels and barked at the moon." Or, "My friend swallowed a tiny rock that she soaked in Holy Water, let it pass, and then buried it when she could see Venus. Two weeks later, no more symptoms."

There are ten thousand stories like this on the Internet. I love it when they say, "If it didn't work, then why did she get better?" Well, she got better because it's a relapsing-remitting disease. It goes away for long periods of time and then comes back with a vengeance. Someone else told me, "You know MS goes away when you're sixty." Okay, well, that gives me something to look forward to in fifteen to twenty years. Ha-ha. We all pray for miracles, but they don't happen that often. If they did, they'd be called "Reality TV."

I started thinking about other encounters I'd had with people who had positive, even inspiring, stories. I once saw a guy in a wheelchair who was wearing a T-shirt that read, I'M NOT HANDI-CAPPED. I'M JUST TIRED. I met a woman at a function who not only had MS, but cerebral palsy, too. She was in one of those stretcher wheelchairs. Everybody in the room knew this woman, and they loved her. She was funny, she was making jokes, and they all gathered around to hear her talk about her son's narcolepsy. I admired her enormously, and I walked away from her thinking, She does not have any self-pity. Not for one minute. In turn, nobody around her felt sorry for her. Even if they did, there was simply no time for it. There's a saying I once heard: Angels fly because they take themselves lightly. In my quest for ways to deal with my illness, that struck the right chord. The stories these people tell aren't about magical cures. They are closer to the truth, and more optimistic. They reminded me of my mother, and of how she loved our circus life, no matter what it brought.

I knew if I became a spokesperson, that would be part of my message—that it wasn't about crazy cures. I could talk about how people react to disease, and how the world changes its attitude toward you. Above all, I could help them learn what my mother always taught me—despite what it doles out, life isn't so bad. It wasn't about giving up on my career, which I wasn't planning on. Rather, it was about making the best of what I had.

So I decided I was finally ready to talk about it. I figured I might as well play myself in front of audiences. The minute I decided to go public, my agents, managers, and masseurs woke from a long slumber. There was press to be had. I was still a little unsure of what I was doing, but I decided to forge ahead.

The publicist from the drug company called up my new best friend, Larry King, and arranged to give him the exclusive first interview in which I'd talk openly about my disease.

In October 2002, I went on *Larry King Live* to talk about my life with MS. I was completely honest about how I felt. I had a positive attitude. In fact, maybe I was a little too positive because Larry seemed dissatisfied. He asked if I was depressed, if I'd cried when I found out. He kept probing, and I kept saying I was fine. I know that isn't provocative, but it was the truth. Larry said, "I'm trying to find some unhappiness here, and you're almost making it sound like: 'Let's all go out and get MS!'" I know it would have been more dramatic for me to be upset, but I stuck with the truth. "I'm fine, I'm okay. I'm just taking it day by day."

I don't do well when I am forced to look at the dark side; who does? I do try to live in the light. I've always been that way. As Shakespeare said, "There is nothing good or bad, but thinking makes it so." Besides, I have a lot of things to be thankful for—a beautiful home, a hell-on-wheels daughter, and a career that has bumbled along an interesting road for many years and still keeps going. And, of course, the Beatles.

I may not be able to do all the things I used to be able to do. I used to do fifty things a day (and when I say fifty, I mean eight). I'd run around like a centipede mamboing on a griddle of hot chicken fat. Now I prioritize. I do maybe four things a day (and by that I mean one). I pick and choose what's most important, and as long as twisting off a bottle cap or climbing eight hundred stairs isn't one of them, I'm fine. I have to admit that sometimes I dream about being Sylvester Stallone in *Rocky*, about running up the stairs in Philadelphia, waving my fists in triumph. I miss dancing my heart out. I miss being able to walk like I used to. I miss my days as the Italian Stallion.

22

Keep Your Chins Up

After the publicity blitz surrounding my announcement that I had MS, my job as a spokesperson for Serono went into full swing. It turned out to be one of the greatest jobs I ever had. I attended MS seminars called MS In Balance, where a doctor would explain the scientific data about MS, after which I'd give my hilarious (yes, you heard me) thirty-minute speech about living with MS. For the first time in my life, I got to play myself all the time. And the character of me was going to need a lot of expensive costumes.

I loved the idea of trying to make even a small difference in someone's life. Hopefully, my stories would help other people with MS connect, and make them smile. I thought I could show what a difference a positive attitude could make. I thought people could benefit from that. In conjunction with drugs and medical treatment, a positive attitude and a sense of humor go a long way. In fact, more and more, science is discovering this to be true.

As I stood at the podium to give my first speech, I looked at the crowd of people in front of me. More women than men, old, young, in business clothes and in jeans. Slender canes punctuated the rows of chairs like exclamation points, and there was a scattering of wheelchairs. This crowd had its own appeal. They were real people—people from all walks of life. But there was more than that to this crowd. These were people who shared something very personal with me. They all had MS, or were there to support their friends and loved ones who did. I'd been to a few MS events in the past, but this time it really hit me. All the craziness of my body wasn't my own singular nightmare. These people knew what I'd been through. They weren't all shooting movies while they struggled with their symptoms, but they were filing law briefs and having children and waiting tables and paying bills and trying to make their lives whole as they fought their own armies of symptoms. I know it's a cliché, but I wasn't alone.

I hadn't known what to expect in giving my first talk. Would I feel exposed and vulnerable? No. It felt nothing like that. It felt like I was conquering years of mystery and misdiagnosis. The first time I gave the speech, I knew it had worked. I was making a connection with this audience, my MS peers, or "my peeps," as I like to call them. There are certain things that might sound shocking to a civilian audience (non-MSers), but with these people there was a real, honest camaraderie. We could laugh about tripping on the corners of rugs and similar mishaps. Not only was I making people laugh, I was feeling better myself. I think it was because I didn't have to explain myself to them. They understood me, and I understood them. This stage performance wasn't about acting, it was about truth.

In my speeches, I tell the audience that when I meet scientists and researchers who are working on a cure for MS, I always tell them to leave no stone unturned. I quote Norman Vincent Peale and say, "You should always shoot for the moon, because even if you don't get there, you get a lot of other good stuff along the way." (Look, they were researching high blood pressure when they discovered Viagra. I'm sure a lot of you men are happy about that. And I'm not unhappy about it.) I wrap up my speech by thanking people for coming and telling them I hope to see them on the way to the moon.

My body had given me a great life, and now it was time for my mind and my spirit to return the favor by sharing my feelings with others. But it was more than that. For all my life I'd loved being onstage, and it was about more than being the center of attention. I wanted to perform, to do what I did best, to use my voice and body to tell a story, and, in doing so, to engage the people who watched me. The skills I had learned as an actor came in handy in my new career.

My mother died a few weeks before I began my effort to educate people about MS. She never accepted that there was anything wrong with me. How could I have a chronic disease? I was her perfect child! We buried her with her tap shoes and a picture of her and my father on a donkey. At her funeral my brother Phil talked about how she always made something out of nothing. When we were kids, he would find moldy green vegetables in the refrigerator and would go to throw them away, but she would stop him. Since she had grown up during the Depression, she'd tell him to cut off the bad parts and save the rest. She always wanted us to savor the good and to keep going. And that's what I was doing at the MS seminars. In the process, I was finding an extended family. Sure, they didn't think I was perfect in the way my mother did, but they understood me in a way that she never could. The signal from my MS family was coming in loud and clear. It was honest, supportive, and hopeful.

After the first event, I had dinner with my new friends from Serono. They told me that the crowd had liked me, and how happy they were. Then they started talking about my tour schedule, where the events were, when I had to show up, and what my responsibilities were. My contract was for a year. I'd never had a job that actually lasted for a year before, for fear of being smothered. Even though we gypsies like to keep our options open, this new job was really fulfilling. I could still act, of course. I planned to keep acting. But I didn't have to.

So I went on the road for MS LifeLines. I fly from Sioux Falls, South Dakota, to Boston to Houston to Tacoma, Washington. The seminars usually take place in hotel banquet halls. The doctor kicks off the seminars by explaining all the medicines available and how they work, including the drug I use, Rebif. He shows slides of the brain and presents lots of medical theory about where MS might come from (they still don't know). Then, after the doctor and nurse take questions from the audience, it's time for me. First they show film clips from my old movies (to remind people of what I've done). Then, I talk about my semihumorous experiences with MS, how I got a diagnosis, and how my life is now, and I throw in a few jokes about George Bush just to keep things on the up-and-up. We take questions as a panel, and after that comes my favorite part: I mingle with the audience, exchanging stories and learning about how other people with MS feel about what's happening. Most of it is pretty damn funny.

Odd things happen on the road. Several times I've run into ex-boyfriends or guys I had crushes on in high school. One old crush in Utah had been married five times and couldn't remember if I was one of them. In Buffalo, there was a *Star Trek* fan convention at the same hotel, and a bunch of Spocks came up to me to talk about the episode I was in. I later assured my audience that we may have MS, but at least we live on planet Earth. On the way to an event in Cleveland, the door fell off my limo and the driver refused to continue with no door, so I had to hitchhike to the event. (Nothing but the best for Miss Garr.) Once, when I was in Las Vegas giving a talk at Green Valley Ranch Resort, I found myself standing next to a slot machine that had a photo of me from *Young Frankenstein* on it. I promptly lost $25 in quarters paying tribute to my own image. And when I had an ear infection and couldn't fly, I made an appearance by satellite from my living room. There was a truck with an antenna the size of the Eiffel Tower parked in my driveway all morning. Apparently, they don't have the satellite thing down yet.

When I first started going on the road for MS LifeLines, I brought Molly a souvenir from every city. I started with T-shirts, but when her drawers filled up with unworn T-shirts saying things like GET SILLY IN PHILLY, I downgraded to snow globes, then mugs. Now I just call her and say, "I'm on my way home, honey. Your present is that we get to be together. Now do your homework." During the summer or when Molly's on vacation, she'll come with me and make her own appearance. I hand her the microphone and she says, "My mom is just a regular person. She's my mom." I'm glad she doesn't have much to say about having a mother with MS. That's how it should be.

Once I started traveling so much, I really had to learn to budget my time. I was performing regularly, and I was being the best mother I could be. I was on medication that was proven to slow the progression of my disease, and my progression was indeed nice and slow. I was getting used to my diagnosis, and talking about how MS changed my life in ways that I never thought it would. It felt good.

I started paying attention to the new community I'd entered— not just the audiences, but the individuals in those audiences. The petite, shy woman named Ellen who came up to me afterward to say, "My daughter Tanya was diagnosed and she won't talk about how she feels. She doesn't want to deal with it. But when I saw that you were speaking, she said that she would come. She knew you as Phoebe's mother on *Friends*. We've been dealing with the physical issues, but after listening to you she's agreed to talk to a therapist. Thank you." It seemed that I was putting my celebrity to good use. One thing I've noticed after doing so many of these events is that most people gravitate to a one-liner philosophy that works best for them. In Philly I met a young woman named Julie in her midthirties. Julie had decided that MS wasn't a hardship but rather an opportunity to learn how strong she was. She and I were cut from the same cloth. In San Francisco a man who was about my age told me that he felt MS helped him rediscover how much he loved life. For him, it was a new beginning. Another one of my peeps, Ashley, a middle-aged homemaker in Texas, told me that her MS made the whole family slow down. It brought them closer together and taught them how to appreciate one another. It amazed me how many people found the good in the bad. They each found a way to survive.

There's a joke I sometimes tell in my speeches. It goes like this: A guy sees a sign that reads, TALKING DOG FOR SALE in front of a house. He knocks on the door, asks to see the dog, and is sent around to the backyard. A dog is sitting there. The man says hi to the dog, and the dog says, "You know, I've had quite a life. I worked for the CIA, spent some time in Washington counseling the president, then had stints at the FBI and NASA. Later I deployed some missiles in Saudi Arabia." The man is very impressed. He goes back to the front porch and says to the owner, "What do you want for that dog back there?" The owner says, "Ten bucks." The guy says, "Ten bucks? But he's such an amazing dog!" And the owner says, "Well . . . he's a big, fat liar."

After I told this joke at one of my talks, I got a letter from a lawyer who has MS. No, he wasn't suing me for telling bad jokes. He said that the dog joke had changed his life. He'd really taken it to heart. It reminded him to make the best of what he had. Now he tells it at all of his board meetings. He used these exact words: "Thank you. You changed my life."

I've learned that my words and jokes can help others who are struggling to keep their spirits dancing, while their bodies dance to another song entirely. Bruce Springsteen has a song called "Land of Hope and Dreams" in which he says, "You'll need a good companion for this part of the ride." The people I meet who have MS are my companions. We give each other hope. I had no idea that talking to people about MS would change me. I thought I would go out there, tell my MS story, and encourage people to keep their chins up. Now I realize it's not a one-way street. I love to remind them that with hope, they can move on in the face of this disease. Maybe what I say doesn't help everyone. We all have our own ways of dealing with life's challenges. But what I know for sure is that it always helps to find a community of people who understand what you're going through, to find comfort and sympathy in the company of new friends.

Ultimately, I have come to the conclusion that I am not defined by this disease. I'm defined by my spirit and by what's inside of me.

23

The Little Engine That Could

As I faced my diagnosis and delved into the reality of it, my marriage began to unravel. Try as we might, John and I couldn't seem to get it together. By now you know that I can always pick the handsome dysfunctional Irish guy out of a room of saints, and John was brought up by a mom who ironed his underwear, not something I could do. Oh, I would if I could, but I just can't. It's against my religion. Some days I thought he expected me to have dinner on the table for him every night, and that's all it would have taken to make him happy. But he would have been better off with a Stepford wife than with me.

The other thing that posed a problem in our marriage was that I was extremely fatigued. I could never get enough sleep. He didn't understand that. He thought I was just lazy and was frustrated when I slept through breakfast and then couldn't bring myself to stay up past six. I often slept twelve hours a night, and if I didn't, I'd need a two-hour nap. What we didn't know at the time was that fatigue is one of the biggest symptoms of MS.

We both loved our four-year-old daughter, and we were focused on her happiness and healthy development, but the truth was that we'd lived separately until Molly was born, and we were happier that way. We got along much better with a little distance between us, and we both realized it almost immediately. I have to say, it's amazing how well our marriage worked out as soon as we figured this out and split up.

It wasn't easy at first. John was living in Valencia, thirty miles north of L.A., and I'd go there every week to pick up Molly. But we had unresolved issues, and I was always afraid there'd be a fight. Luckily, Alfa-Betty and Marshall were in town that first winter, and they would drive with me to pick up Molly. On the ride home there was always terrible traffic and Marshall, who claimed he'd never met a baby before in his life, would sing songs to cheer Molly up, try to distract her from the reality of her future: endless miles of L.A. traffic.

Despite the crap John and I went through, I always remember that he is a good father. He takes Molly camping, skiing, fly-fishing—all the things I regretfully have to pass on. I try to make amends by learning state capitals and mastering third-grade math. (Okay, I'll *never* master third-grade math, or algebra for that matter, but the capital of Delaware is Dover.)

One MS study I read reported that the rate of divorce is higher among those marriages in which the woman has MS. In my travels, I meet tons of women who tell me, "My husband left me when I got my diagnosis of MS." I say to them, "Good riddance to bad rubbish." Most people just aren't prepared for a health crisis, no matter how much they might love each other. It's tough.

Maybe the wedding vows should say, "In sickness, including but not limited to MS and other chronic diseases, 'til death do us part."

On the other hand, once a woman came up to me and said, "I am so lucky because my husband didn't leave me when I got my diagnosis of MS." Why give the guy a medal? I thought love was love was love. My relationship with John was more than worth the trouble of its demise, however. Molly has been the greatest joy of my life. Everything is much more important because of her. At the writing of this book she's eleven years old and a whirlwind of imagination. She has brown hair, brown eyes, a round Irish face, and freckles. I tried to send her to dance and piano classes, but she prefers camping, fishing, baseball, and volleyball. And her father has been taking her skiing every weekend in winter since she was six. She skis for the Mammoth Mountain Ski Team, the number one ski team in the United States. She can't wait till she's thirteen, when she will be eligible to race in the downhill events, where speeds reach upward of eighty miles per hour. Molly was born with a complete lack of fear. (Once, when she was about seven, she saw a boy walk out on an ocean pier railing to the pier's end. She jumped up on the rail and walked out on the railing, too. No boy is going to outdo her!) Every year she has qualified and participated in the U.S. Western Nationals. Oh yes, she's quite the skier so far. I take care of her, and in the process, I take extra good care of myself. She keeps me going in the face of whatever goes on in my body.

I want to make sure that Molly has everything I lacked in my childhood. Doesn't everybody do this? I sometimes go a little overboard. I don't want her to be spoiled, but it's been hard for me to deny her anything. But just recently, when she brought home a rabbit, I told her it couldn't stay. We already have a dog (Cleo), two cats (Charlie and Boo Radley), and two fish (Alfred and Little Alfred). A mother has to draw the line somewhere. Sometimes we have a funny, flip-flopped relationship. She'll say, "Mom, get out of bed." On my worst days I'll say, "I can't," to which she replies, "You can." And she's right. To say that I have a relapsing-remitting disease of the central nervous system would be Pig Latin to her. She just knows that sometimes I'm weak and some-times I'm fine. It's very clear-cut to her. And that's how I deal with it, too. I can't predict how I'll feel tomorrow—who can?—but I know how I feel at that moment. Thank God (if She's up there) I have Molly to keep me on track and to help me keep my perspective on what really matters.

Last summer Molly and I went to the Hollywood Bowl for the Fourth of July Spectacular with my friend Heidi and her thirteen-year-old daughter, Haley. The L.A. Philharmonic was playing. As usual, I overpacked. The four of us headed to our seats with our picnic basket, cooler, and a bunch of crap we really didn't need—blankets, pillows, umbrellas, a portable massage table (kidding). Well, the hike to the seats ended up being a lot longer than we had imagined, and it was about eighty-five degrees. I was limping a lit-tle when we spotted one of those drive-around-the-parking-lot electric golf carts. I thought, My prince has come! I stuck out my thumb in the universal gesture of Dude, I need a ride, and the well-built, unemployed actor/groundskeeper said, "I'm not going your way," and zoomed past us. I guess I looked better than I felt. I wasn't looking for sympathy; I just wanted a ride.

The heat was killing me, and pretty soon I fell down, right on my butt, in front of all the concertgoers. The kids laughed, and so did I. I fall frequently enough that it isn't a huge deal. Just then an usher saw us and offered to send somebody. We waited and waited, but nobody ever came. Determined not to give up, I started up the road again. We were on a steep hill, carting all our stuff. Why did I have to bring the seventeen-pound roasted turkey? All of a sudden Molly and Haley started chanting, "I think I can, I think I can, I think I can, I know I can, I know I can . . ." My daughter bounced as she sang, full of life. I felt a surge of strength. All four of us sang along as we transformed into the little engines that could.

It made me feel so much better. Just as we were almost to the top of the hill, Molly, in her eleven-year-old loving way, had a change of heart and said, "Mom, stop singing, you're embarrassing me!" As I looked around I realized everyone could hear us being the little engines that could. It mortified Molly, but it didn't embarrass me . . . I'm used to being a bad singer.

It took me a long time to make peace with my life. But now I want to get to the point—no nonsense, I just want to cut to the chase. Maybe it's part of growing older, too. I realize how short life is, and how pure the quality of life should be. The BS about who has the best car or the biggest house is just that—BS. It's all been put in perspective for me. Okay, I'm not going to trade in my car or move out of my house, but having MS *has* put those things in perspective. They're just things.

Yesterday my friend Heidi complained about standing in a grocery-store line for ten minutes. Heidi and I don't let each other get away with anything. I told her, "Who cares? So you have to wait in a grocery line. Wait or don't wait, but why spend as much time complaining as you spent in the line? It just doubles the wasted time." You know the mantra by now, dear reader: Kwitcher Bitchin'. I try to do as my mother taught me and roll with the punches. Ten-minute lines end. Make the best of your time—grab an *Enquirer* and find out about which alien stole whose baby.

Recently, Molly's fifth-grade class was going to take a field trip to Olvera Street, in the oldest part of Los Angeles. It's a classic school trip that every fifth-grader in L.A. takes to learn the history of this colorful Mexican marketplace. Molly asked if I would be one of the chaperones. I said yes, but I honestly thought she would forget about it. Well, she didn't. Next thing you know, she said, "Okay, our trip to Olvera Street is next week, and I told the teacher you would like to go." What could I say? Then the teacher called me up and said, "Molly said you're interested in being a chaperone on our field trip. That's great!"

I said, "Isn't that a cobblestone street? I don't know if I can do it. Walking up and down that street with a bunch of high-energy, wound-up kids? I don't know if I'm the best person for the job."

She chuckled and said, "Well, there are three other chaperones. You'll only have four kids each."

I felt lame making excuses, but I said, "I still think it's going to be too hard. I can't do it. I'm sorry."

To which she replied, "You get a free lunch." Doesn't she know there's no such thing as a free lunch in Hollywood? I said no. Cut to one hour later. When Molly gets frustrated with her schoolwork (math's a breeze, but reading can be tricky), I'm the one who always tells her that she can do anything she sets her mind to, and that she should keep trying.

I thought about this and called her teacher back. "Hello, Ms. Rea, it's Teri Garr. I think I would like to go to Olvera Street. I am always telling my daughter that she has to try stuff, and I'm not setting a very good example if I don't go. I'm in."

So I got on the school bus and rode to Olvera Street with five thousand screaming kids. I hadn't been on a bus in God knows how many years. Those seats are hard! When we got to Olvera Street I wasn't the world's most desirable chaperone. Not only was I slower, I was having a hard time finding all the items on their scavenger hunt. Why did they have to do that? Couldn't we just look at the candles and eat tacos? Even though I was stumbling a little and moving slower than everybody else, I thought it was good for Molly's friends to see me like this, the way I really was.

I'm fine. And Molly lives with me, and she's fine. It isn't every day you get to teach a bunch of fifth-graders a life lesson. The bus ride, the walk, the kids—it all exhausted me, but ultimately the entire Olvera Street experience was good, and so was the gua-camole. The biggest lesson I learned was that I can pretty much sleep anywhere, including on a school bus, riding back from a long day with a bunch of screaming kids. I'm glad I stood by my words: "You have to try."

As I write this, I look around and realize that I'm living my childhood fantasy—the one I acted out on that Houston Street porch in North Hollywood when I was nine years old. I have a baby and a house and girlfriends and lots of clothes—and no man!

One day I couldn't unscrew a cap off a bottle. I thought, Wow, my hand is a mess today. Then I realized that I couldn't undo bot-tle caps *before* I had MS. So there! Things are hard for a perfectly healthy person sometimes, too. Everyone's life, at some point, feels like a childproof cap: It should be a whole lot easier than it is, but for whatever reason it isn't. Like my friend Gilda Radner used to say, "It's always something." If I were to believe "I am my ill-ness," I'd have a long road ahead of me, and no map.

Don't get me wrong. I have my share of pity parties. But they don't last very long. I've got them down to twenty minutes at a time. I set the kitchen timer and feel sorry for myself for twenty minutes. No more, no less. Life sucks/why me/can't a girl get a break in this town/why are tomatoes so expensive these days? And, of course, why the hell did the Beatles break up? When the buzzer goes off, I'm done.

Epilogue

Gotta Dance

I play FreeCell on the computer for hours. I mean *hours*. Sometimes, if Molly is with her dad or if she has gone to bed, I will play for four hours without blinking an eye. If I were knitting sweaters, I'd have five hundred. But I live in Los Angeles, and who needs sweaters in L.A.? Sometimes when I'm out at a party, I catch myself thinking, I can't wait to get home and play FreeCell on the computer. Ah, the glamorous life of an actress. FreeCell is all about organizing. A whole deck of cards is thrown out on the table and you have to put it in the proper order, somehow, moving one card at a time. It feels so good when I do it right. It may sound crazy, but it puts me back in control. That's one of the challenges of MS—lack of control. I constantly have to reorganize my life to accommodate my fluctuating needs. Playing on the computer for hours isn't the best way of doing it, but it really does help me. I love the metaphor, making order from chaos.

While I'm playing, somewhere in the back of my mind I'm

working things out. Or at least that's my latest justification for wasting hours and hours on the computer. It's so simple, so solitary. There is no one telling me I am right or wrong, and there's no gray area, either. I either win or lose.

One of the questions I am forever contemplating when it comes to MS is this: Why do people think having MS means you're on your way out? I met a woman from Nebraska who said she was diagnosed with MS at thirty-one, when she already had two little children. Her kids grew up, went to college, and she and her husband built a handicapped-accessible house for their retirement, just in case. They always had it in the back of their minds that the MS would get worse, but it didn't. She hadn't felt any symptoms for about eight years, so she went for a checkup, got an MRI, and the neurologist told her, "It's gone." Now that sounds like a miracle to me. She said the doctor looked at all her medical records from twenty-five years ago, including her spinal tap, and actually said, "This is amazing." She is thrilled and she laughed as she told me, but she's still not totally convinced. "MS can pull fast ones," she told me. But stories like that keep us all going.

We don't make the rules. One of the only things we can control about any affliction—and life in general—is our attitude toward dealing with it. I've never met anyone with perfect health, a perfect marriage, perfect kids, and a perfect life. If you're alive you've likely got issues, and still you find a way to lead a productive life. I remember the words of an eighty-four-year-old friend of mine who has had MS for fifty years. Over time she's decided that it's just a lifelong annoyance. That is one of the best things I've ever heard about MS, and it's the way I have chosen to deal with it—an annoyance that I've learned to live with, like bunions. It may not be pleasant, but it's a part of who I am.

When I think back on my days in New York City, I miss my jogs in Central Park. I miss my long walks up and down Broadway, looking in all the windows, spending money on shoes. I miss dancing, but I wouldn't be dancing much at my age, anyway. I can't do that anymore. I walk two blocks and I'm exhausted and ready to take a cab. But if I were walking, I'd be shopping, spending money and buying stuff I don't need. Now, instead, I take time to read, to be quiet, and to enjoy being in one place. I was always so hyper. Now I enjoy my daughter, my friends, peacefulness, and, of course, FreeCell.

When I work, I plan in advance so I'll have the energy I need. When I have to give a speech or do an interview or write something, I make room for it. I don't have endless stores of energy, but who does? I just plan ahead and try to remember to be kind to myself—shouldn't everybody?

Of all the people with disabilities, 98 percent of them say they started to appreciate life so much more after they learned that there was something wrong with them. I actually consider myself lucky sometimes. I now appreciate the things I do have rather than the things I don't have. I have my family, and a house overrun with kids and various animals, chaos, and lots of old and new friends. To appreciate life seems obvious, but sometimes we need to have an anvil dropped on a foot before we realize it.

I really do count my blessings. At least I used to; now I get so tired, I have a woman come in once a week and count them for me. But really, I've learned to slow down a lot. I needed a rest from the breakneck speed I'd always maintained. Nothing would have slowed me down, I'm certain of it, not even speedbumps. I finally have time to connect with the people around me, to listen to Green Day with Molly, to go to Disneyland, and even to ride the

Mummy roller coaster at the Universal Studios Hollywood Amusement Park (big mistake, by the way). I now know it's important to have time to have fun.

A while ago, Gregory Hines's death hit me like a rock to my head. He was the stuff that legends are made of—a charming, graceful, one-of-a-kind dancer. He died of cancer at fifty-seven. People were shocked; nobody even knew he was sick. My heart went out to all who loved him. But at the same time I thought, Well, good for him. He didn't let his illness become his life. He danced till he died. That's what I've always wanted to do. And you know what? Something in me is gonna dance till I die. It might be a different dance than the one I was trained to do, it may be just my spirit dancing, but I'll be dancing just the same.

Acknowledgments

Let me just take a moment to thank a few of my friends, relatives, and enemies who helped me get through the wild experience of writing a book. I wasn't sure I could do it, so I really am grateful.

Let me start with the ground floor. Henriette Mantel, the genius or should I say semi-genius, who talked me into doing this in the first place. Without her help I would never have pulled myself away from my FreeCell games. We also had quite a few laughs reviewing my sordid little life. I so appreciate her pristine Vermont sensibilities, and her innate irreverence to anything that's labeled normal. They straightened my ass out. Thanks, Hen.

Next I want to thank the actual book people who made this whole thing happen. They include the gentle, tough, and brilliant Lydia Wills, the persistent, imaginative, and patient Laureen Rowland, and our special angel, Hilary Lifton. Their unwavering support kept us going.

A special thanks to some old friends and relatives who helped me remember some long-forgotten stories: Marshall Efron, Alfa Betty Olsen, Anne Marshall, Toni Basil, Howard Franklin, Stuart Cornfeld, and of course my brothers Ed and Phil and their families.

I'd like to thank Merrill Markoe for pointing out that there is so much information about MS on the Internet that reviewing it can sometimes be a bigger pain in the butt than actually having it. Thanks to Bill Taylor, Steve Skrovan, Mark Ebner, Francis Gasparini, Michael Patrick King, Lynn Tierney, Jonathan Katz, and the lovely Cheryl Bricker. You know what you did. Thanks to Paul Slansky, Liz Dubelman, and Arleen Sorkin for always encouraging me and telling me I could indeed be a writer. I hope they're right.

My unending gratitude to Lyndi Hirsch, Ken O'Flarity, Harriet Sternberg, and the rest of the gang at Serono for all your help. Thanks to Marc Gurvitz at Brillstein Grey, and to Camille Kuznetz, the real brains behind that operation. Special thanks to BB and Dan Mcleod for their ever-faithful support and love.

My life wouldn't be complete without the licking, whining, barking, meowing, and loving of Cleo, Charlie, Bo Radley, Midge, Buckmaster Trouble, Betty Rainbow, and Roxie, a various selection of animals that listened to Henriette and me during this process and on many occasions, nodded their approval. Thanks to John O'Neil for being such a great dad to Molly and to Molly for keeping her room clean (hint, hint).

And last but not least I want to thank Rosa Diaz, whose heart and soul always inspire me and without whom Molly and I would never get to school on time.

About the Author

Teri Garr is one of Hollywood's most beloved comic actresses, starring in such classic films as *Young Frankenstein; Oh, God!; Close Encounters of the Third Kind; Mr. Mom; After Hours;* and *Tootsie,* for which she received an Academy Award nomination for Best Supporting Actress. Trained as a dancer, early in her career Teri performed with several ballet companies and went on to dance on television and in films, several with Elvis Presley. In the seventies, she became a well-known television personality with appearances on shows such as *Star Trek, That Girl,* and *The Andy Griffith Show,* and as a regular on *The Sonny and Cher Comedy Hour.* In the late nineties, she played the mother of television's most popular ditz—Phoebe (played by Lisa Kudrow)—on NBC's hit sitcom *Friends.*

In October 2002, Teri announced on national television that she had multiple sclerosis. Since then, she has become a leading advocate in raising awareness for MS and the latest treatments for the disease, and has won several awards for her dedication and

service. Teri travels around the United States and Canada on be-
half of Serono, Inc. and Pfizer, Inc, the manufacturers of Rebif,
the MS drug she takes, speaking to corporations, physicians, and
patients about her experience. She is also the national chair of the
Multiple Sclerosis Society's Women Against MS program.

When she's not on the road, Teri resides in Los Angeles with
her daughter, Molly; a dog; two cats; and seventeen goldfish.